Calligraphy with PHOTOSHOP

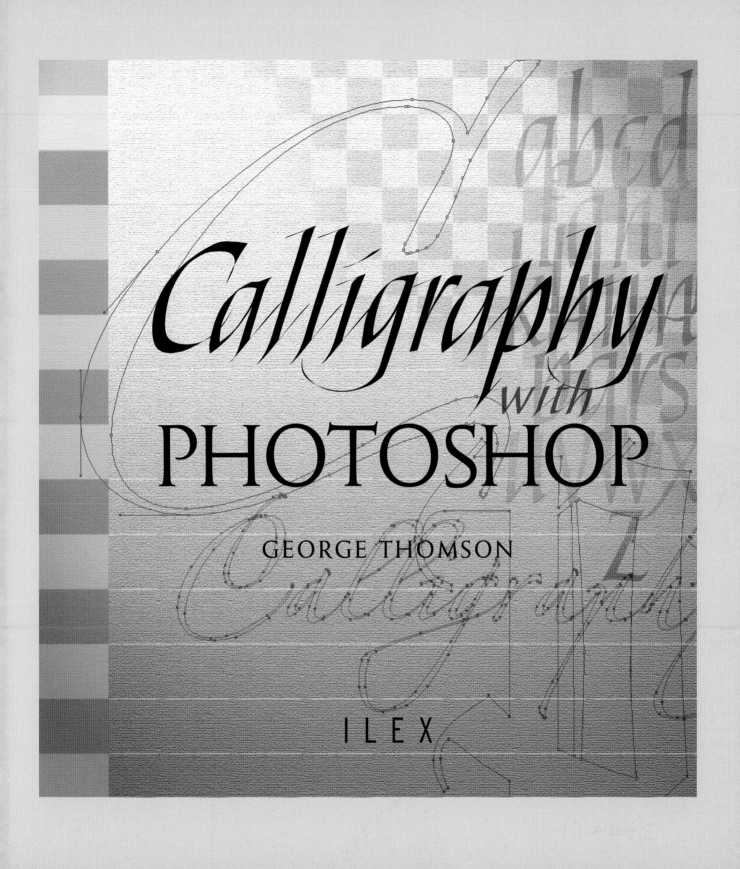

Calligraphy

with

PHOTOSHOP

GEORGE THOMSON

ILEX

First published in the United Kingdom in 2004 by

ILEX

The Old Candlemakers
West Street
Lewes
East Sussex BN7 2NZ

ILEX is an imprint of The Ilex Press Ltd
Visit us on the web at:
www.ilex-press.com

ILEX Editorial, Lewes:
Publisher: Alastair Campbell
Executive Publisher: Sophie Collins
Creative Director: Peter Bridgewater
Editorial Director: Steve Luck
Editor: Ben Renow-Clarke
Design Manager: Tony Seddon
Designer: Andrew Milne
Artwork Assistant: Joanna Clinch

ILEX Research, Cambridge:
Commissioning Editor: Alan Buckingham
Development Art Director: Graham Davis
Technical Art Editor: Nicholas Rowland

British Library Cataloguing-in-Publication Data
A catalogue record for this book is available
from the British Library

ISBN 1-904705-54-5

Printed and bound in China

For more information on this title please visit:
www.capsuk.web-linked.com

354481

Contents

INTRODUCTION

Calligraphy: the contemporary scene

6

At the time of the Renaissance three great Italian scribes produced books that were to influence calligraphy and introduce the art of writing to anyone who could afford to purchase them. Ludovico Arrighi's *La Operina* (1522), Giouanniantonio Tagliente's *Lo presente libro Insegn*a (1530), and Giovanbattista Palatino's *Libro Nuovo* (1540) were 'copybooks' that demonstrated how to write in the italic hand. The production of these works was achieved with the process of relief printing. This is not the revolutionary method of printing by movable type developed by Gutenberg in about 1450, by which it was impossible to reproduce a calligraphic style, but a much simpler process that had been used for centuries before. The originals of the writing masters were copied by an engraver and cut in wood blocks from which the books were printed.

Following the works of these master scribes, many copybooks were printed in Europe and America. For the first time, technology and calligraphy had met and the ensuing centuries saw the use of 'new technologies' in the way these manuals were produced, including the change to printing from copperplates, which not only greatly improved the reproduction quality, but also significantly influenced the letterforms.

Per che' formandole di quadro perfetto,
Verrebbono (quanto alla pro-
portione de'l corpo) mer-
cantili; & non
Cancellaresche.
Et questa misura si hauerà tirando un
parallelo ò uolemo dir due' linee
dritte' discosta l'una da l'altra
à giuditio de l'occhio
(Secondo la grandezza che'uorete
de la lettera) in questa
maniera

Dipoi le attrauersarete' si che'le
due' trauerse' siano di-
stanti fra loro

Left Palatino was considered to be the greatest of the three Italian Renaissance writing masters. This is from his book Libro Nuovo *(1540).*

Left A restrained flourish from Tagliente's Lo presente libro Insegna *(1530).*

Below Formal computer-aided calligraphy.

AN UAIR DH'ÉIRE
GINN AN T·ABH·
AIL

'S 'N UAIR A THUI·
TEAMAID LE ION·
SLUGAIDH·SIOS 'S
NA GLEANNTAIBH
BHEIRTEADH GACH
SEÓL A BHÍODH
AICE AM BÁRR NAN
CRANN DITH

WHEN THE SHIP WAS POISED ON WAVE CREST
IN PROUD FASHION
IT WAS NEEDFUL TO STRIKE SAIL
WITH QUICK PRECISION
WHEN THE VALLEYS NEARLY SWALLOWED US
BY SUCTION
WE FED HER CLOTH TO TAKE HER UP TO
RESURRECTION

It is now obvious that computers play an important role in the lives of almost all of us. The term 'new technology', coined in the late 1960s, is now an anachronism. Although it was usually applied to developing computer-related products, it is arguable whether or not its precise meaning was ever really understood. It was a long time before more than a very few artists and designers saw the potential of these machines, perhaps inhibited, or intimidated, by the need for laborious and time-consuming programming. The development of a graphical user interface in 1968, which made it much easier for the user to communicate with the computer, was a big step forward. Even then artists were slow to embrace the technology. There were still several restricting factors, not least the difficulty and cost of producing good colour prints.

While military applications drove the very earliest computer graphics developments, computer games led the way to more accessible computer systems, ever increasing power, and improved image quality. Designers were provided with software that made their job much easier and enabled them to be creative in ways that had been impossible before. Digital image and print technology developments revolutionized graphic design and printing.

Calligraphy

Calligraphy

Above *Palatino bold italic changed to a condensed outline form with Macromedia Fontographer.*

INTRODUCTI

Below *Fontographer, and software like it, enabled designers to modify and design typefaces much more easily than had been the case before.*

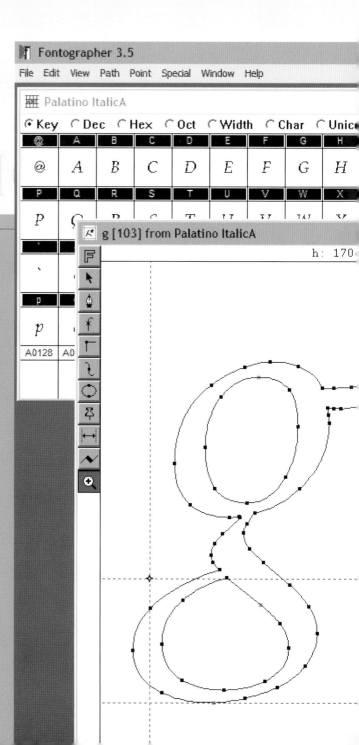

8

Some software that could modify and create lettering came onto the market. Specialized font design software, such as Fontographer and Font Studio, could easily modify existing typefaces and create new ones. Designers woke up to the idea that they were no longer restricted to 'hand lettering' or available fonts and could develop or create their own, often without any real understanding of good letterform. The consequence of all this was that the distinction between the calligraphy of calligraphers and the script lettering of designers was blurred. As happened in the Renaissance, technology had played a part in the evolution of calligraphy and the way in which it was viewed.

Although the number is increasing, very few calligraphers use computers in their work. Perhaps this is because many scribes perceive calligraphy as a craft, steeped in traditional values. Much discussion and argument has taken place over the last twenty years or so on the acceptability of calligraphy that is more akin to fine art than to the traditional craft, with its conventions of legibility and technical excellence. But should we not welcome creativity and celebrate the calligraphic marks that we make, whether or not they make words or sentences that we can read? Calligraphy in Japan and

Below *Photoshop opens up a realm of calligraphic possibilities that are unachievable with pen and ink. The gradient on this lettering is a prime example.*

China has done so for centuries. Computer calligraphy ranges from formal text to totally abstract art. If calligraphy performs the function it is designed to do, whether this is within a formal document or a visually exciting, but totally illegible, creative piece, and this is communicated to the viewer, then are arguments of right and wrong not rather frivolous?

Adobe Photoshop grew out of ideas by Thomas and John Knoll in 1987 that culminated in the release of version 1.0 for the Macintosh in February 1990. Later that year version 2.0 was released. The first version for Windows appeared in April 1993. The latest offering, at the time of writing, is version 8.0, shipped as part of Adobe's Creative Suite and labelled Photoshop CS. Over the years the software has had to take account of major developments in computing, especially the Internet, now handled by an integrated application called ImageReady, and the rapid advances and acceptability of digital photography. Of course Photoshop is not the only high-end image creation, manipulation, and enhancement program but in recent years it has beaten off its rivals, especially Corel PhotoPaint, and is now most widely accepted as the 'industry standard'.

It is not always easy to tell which software application has been used for a piece of work. As we will see in this book, Photoshop excels in what it offers to enable the user to manipulate shape and colour and to create an infinite range of special effects. Although it includes some functionality with vectors, this is very limited. It is not a vector-based program and the calligrapher would be much better off using Adobe Illustrator or CorelDraw for this purpose. Consequently, this book introduces Photoshop as a creative tool that will enhance the creative potential of calligraphers and others who want to explore calligraphic imagery. It suggests several ways of getting calligraphy into the software or generating it directly within the program, but then explains more fully how these ideas can be developed into an exciting, creative art form.

Right *Admirable sentiments and highly skilled calligraphy, but copybooks such as A Delightful Recreation for the Industrious by William Brooks (1717) led to characterless handwriting.*

Below *A page from Edward Johnston's writing sheets Manuscript and Inscriptional Lettering for Schools and Classes.*

INTRODUCTION

From paper to the digital image

It was probably the poet John Milton in the middle of the seventeenth century who first used the term 'calligraphy', but it was not widely used until the nineteenth century. Calligraphy, literally translated from the Greek *kallos* and *graphein*, is 'beautiful writing' or 'writing as an art'. Although the labels are different now, calligraphy can be traced back to the days of the Pharaohs, with their papyrus manuscripts written in scripts called hieratic and demotic. These were written with a pen cut to a broad, chisel-shaped tip, creating thick and thin strokes. The Romans also wrote with a reed pen cut in a similar way. Their rustic capitals show how the letters were affected by the writing instrument. Uncials and half-uncials of the Dark Ages were written on vellum or parchments, animal skins treated to form a smooth writing surface. The letterforms of this period, especially in the seventh and eighth centuries, were very round and did not have the 'ascenders' and 'descenders' with which we are familiar. These first appeared in the Carolinian minuscule, a script that is the basis of the lowercase letters that we now use, alongside 'roman' capitals. While medieval manuscripts with various Gothic styles, including black letter, Rotunda, and Textura, were predominant in central, western, and northern Europe,

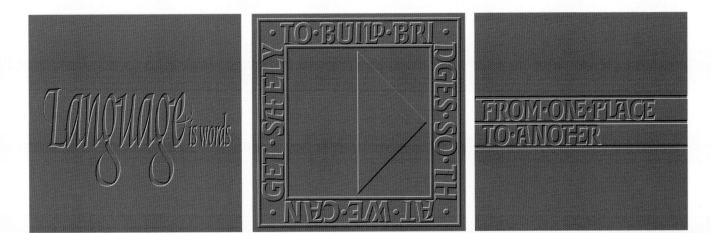

11

scribes in Italy and the south more frequently used a 'humanist' script form that developed into the Renaissance italic and was used in the printed copybooks.

Over the centuries the pure italic form degenerated through the influence of the engraver, who imparted his stylistic variations and flourishes on the letters of the penmen. By the beginning of the nineteenth century writing had become characterless, often overexuberant, although frequently written with great technical skill.

The revival of calligraphy is largely due to William Morris and Edward Johnston, who studied early manuscripts and rediscovered the broad-edged pen as a writing instrument. The influence of Johnston can still be seen in calligraphy today. Calligraphy has become a very popular pastime, with large numbers of individuals participating.

This is evidenced by the many books available and the rise of calligraphy societies and clubs, especially in the USA. It is an art or craft that is relatively inexpensive to pursue and one in which, with guidance and practice, it is possible to reach a level of skill equal to that of the professionals.

Professional trained calligraphers are thin on the ground and, as we have seen, of their number a very small percentage use computers in their work. Those who do work in a variety of ways, an indication of how undeveloped this approach is. Some calligraphers use computers simply as a means of retouching lettering, perhaps in advance of printing. Others go to the other extreme and their calligraphy is 'virtual', to be looked at only on a computer monitor, never touching paper at any point of its creation or output.

MFXVI

Left *A broad-edged pen or brush was used to write Roman rustic capitals, and gives a distinctive style.*

Letters

INTRODUCTION

Effects: gimmicks, clichés, or creativity?

Computer-aided calligraphy is not typography. Using script, even calligraphic typefaces such as Palace Script, Lucida, Vivaldi, or Corsova, is not calligraphy, even if such fonts are employed in a highly creative way. Calligraphy has a human touch. It reflects the feelings of the scribe, the love of creating calligraphic forms, and even the defects in his or her skill. When calligraphers write, every letter is different, even if they try to make every 'a', 'b' or 'c' the same. This imparts life to the writing. When writing calligraphy spontaneity is important – a sudden flourish or variant of a letter in response to a raising of the spirits. This is not just a romantic notion. It is part of the human psyche that we have a desire to express ourselves. Japanese and Chinese calligraphy is both an art and a spiritual act and, while not so fully developed in the West, it can be so in our culture.

Perhaps this too is the soul of computer graphics. The ease with which we can create lines, shapes, and images on the computer screen echoes the impulsiveness, even recklessness that makes calligraphy enjoyable. Add to that the spectrum of visual effects that we can impart to calligraphy and that we can employ with it in Photoshop, and we have a working environment conducive to the creation of the most original and exhilarating visual material.

This is not calligraphy
This is not calligraphy
This is not calligraphy
This is not calligraphy

Above *Example of the many available calligraphic typefaces: Palace Script, Lucida, Vivaldi, and Corsova.*

Right *When a calligrapher writes, each letter is written slightly differently.*

image

12

Above *Is this creative calligraphy, art, or cliché? Some Photoshop effects applied to a letter taken from an eighteenth-century copybook together with the original letter.*

Right *'Virtual' calligraphy. This piece is intended to be viewed on the computer screen, not as a print.*

However, this facility raises some very important questions. When is a computer graphics effect a gimmick? When does it become a visual cliché?

Even in the very early days of computer graphics software, when digital image creation was still extremely limited in every regard, artists and designers like myself who had the privilege of experimenting with it began to ask the question 'what is art?' Images the like of which had never been seen before were suddenly very easy to create, but it wasn't long before the same effects were becoming commonplace and instantly recognizable – they had become clichéd. Later, with much more powerful software, the clichéd use of filters such as emboss, pinch/punch, and twirl made much computer graphics somewhat banal.

Filters and other effects in Photoshop should be used with discretion and applied to create a desired effect. This is not to say that you shouldn't experiment with them, but an aesthetic judgment should always be made on the results. Nor should it imply that, because it can be very easy to create a striking visual effect, they should not be used. Examine the results of your experiments and ask objectively whether you have achieved the desired effect. If not, discard the image and try again.

There could be parallels between the seventeenth- and eighteenth-century copybooks with overstylized letterforms and clichéd flourishing, and what could result from the misuse of Photoshop. On the other hand, the rules have not yet been written. The art form of computer calligraphy is very new and all of us can participate in defining it.

The chances are that you already have a computer, possibly with Photoshop installed, together with a range of peripheral devices. Photoshop is able to run on a computer of relatively modest power by today's standards – but will run very slowly at the lower end of the scale. The software is very demanding on computer resources for some of its features, especially the more complex filters. Some of them, on a low-power machine, can take an unacceptable length of time, possibly hours, to complete. If you find that your computer is running the application very slowly, the only really effective solution is to upgrade and add more memory (RAM). However, read the Photoshop manual. This tells you how to allocate memory in the most efficient manner, and how to minimize the memory usage of your computer's operating system. It appears to be a fact of life that with every new version of a piece of software the demands on the computer increase exponentially. This means that earlier versions of Photoshop will run more quickly than the latest ones on the same machine.

HARDWARE
The computer, mouse, and graphics tablet

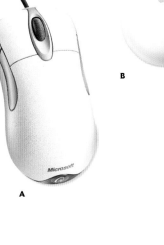

A

B

C

Make sure that you have plenty of space for images. The greater the capacity of your hard disk the better. You will soon fill up 40 gigabytes! A CD writer is a good investment. Most computer systems come with this anyway. Get into the habit of writing your final images, and even experiments, to CDs to conserve the space on your hard disk.

A good monitor is essential. Flat panel LCD screens provide the best display for calligraphic work. Even the best traditional monitors blur the pixels slightly, perhaps an advantage with some types of work. The pixels on an LCD screen are discrete and represent the image more accurately. These monitors also have the great advantage that they take up less space on your desk. A 17-inch monitor showing 1280 × 1024 is the minimum specification for graphic work.

Most calligraphic input will be via a drawing device of some sort – either a mouse or a graphics tablet. A mouse is not a natural tool to write with. However, it is surprising how well it can be used for calligraphy with practice. If you stick with a mouse, it is best to use the infrared type, which is much easier to control. The digital pen, which has buttons, would appear to be a much more natural writing instrument, but it does take some time to adjust to. Most digital pens are pressure-sensitive, drawing a line of greater weight or width with increased pressure, depending on the software. For the greatest control, a fair amount of pressure on the pen is needed to keep the calligraphy in a straight line and consistent slope. Even if you opt for a graphics tablet you will probably find that you will still use your mouse for some graphics operations.

A *A typical infrared mouse. Most mice have a USB connection nowadays, and can be used on both a Macintosh and a PC.*

B *This Macintosh mouse is wireless, giving you more freedom.*

C *Wacom is the industry standard manufacturer of graphics tablets. The larger tablets are not cheap, but then you do not often need a large area for calligraphy. Most tablets come with both a pen and a mouse.*

D *The Wacom Cintiq mixes a graphics tablet with a flat panel display, so that you can write directly onto the screen.*

D

There are three main ways of getting calligraphy onto your computer screen. One is to produce the lettering itself in other software such as Adobe Illustrator or CorelDraw, a method that is beyond the scope of this book. Another is to write the lettering with one of Photoshop's pen or brush tools. Alternatively, calligraphy that you have written on paper can be scanned so that it can be manipulated and modified digitally. Good scanners are now inexpensive, reliable, and can acquire images at a very high resolution, suitable for working with in Photoshop.

If you find it hard to write directly on screen in Photoshop, it could be your salvation! Skilled calligraphers who are moving into the digital world will, almost certainly, choose to work this way and utilize their traditional skills.

Although you may be happy to go no further than storing your calligraphy as digital files to be viewed on screen, a print has a quality that is very different, especially when special papers are used. While laser printers are useful to proof your images in black and white, they are of limited use for the finished output. The exceptions to this are

HARDWARE

Scanners and printers

Above *The colour fidelity of high-end scanners is not a requirement when dealing with calligraphy, as the majority of lettering will be re-coloured, if not re-drawn, on screen.*

Below *The greatest benefits of laser printers are print speed and quality. Speed is not an issue for most calligraphy work, but the quality and consistency of laser printing can be a great boon.*

small-scale print items such as cards, invitations, and even small books. Laser prints have the advantage that they can print double-sided documents successfully, as there is little or no 'shine-through', a drawback of some other processes.

The ubiquitous inkjet printer is a great device for producing the final copy of your calligraphic work. Inkjets can output print that resembles written ink on paper, at very high resolution. The problem of colour permanency, which used to be a serious consideration, is far less so now. Most inks will not fade or change colour for many years. There are specialist archival products that will outlast most colour media. The prints that most users will be able to produce will be rather small (letter or A4). This is somewhat limiting. Printers that will print A3 or, better still, A2 are far more suitable. While this comes at a cost, bear in mind that

you do not need a 'photo' printer, since standard inkjets are satisfactory for calligraphy. You can, of course, use a bureau for very special work, although check that they can print on your choice of paper. Printer manufacturers will tell you a maximum paper thickness that can be used on their machines (usually 80 gm^2). Probably, this is to protect warranties. Provided the paper will actually feed through the machine, the printer should come to no harm.

When buying a printer give some consideration to the cost of consumables. Colour ink cartridges are expensive. Colour accuracy is not often critical for calligraphic work, so the use of cheaper products is worth thinking about. Another option is to use refill kits. However, if your work comprises only lettering and not large areas of solid colour, the amount of ink used for each print will be very small.

Left *Inkjet printers are perfect for most calligraphic work, as they are cheaper than their laser brethren, but still produce good-quality results.*

This is not a book on how to use your computer. Nor is it a book on how to use Photoshop, although the following two pages are provided as a refamiliarization. This is a book on how Photoshop can be used to create and modify calligraphy. Therefore, you should have a working knowledge of all your hardware, including computer and peripherals as well as all the standard menus and commands. Although some aspects of computer files that relate to computer graphics will be covered, you should know how to load and save files and how to organize them in an efficient way. Within Photoshop you should already be familiar with the basic menus, toolbars, and palettes, and have a practical knowledge of working with layers. If you are not at this stage, then spend a little while with the manual and the help screens within the program. If you are entirely new to Photoshop, learn some of the basics first then have some fun trying out ideas in this book. Often the best way to learn is through making mistakes. It costs nothing to try out lots of different ideas.

SOFTWARE

Before you start: what you should know

A *The vast range of filters available in Photoshop are simple to use but can create very effective images, based on calligraphy, that look much more complex than they really are.*

B *Photoshop lets you work with vectors to change the shape of letters. However, since this is not its primary function, the procedures can be a bit fiddly. For example, anchor points are very small and must be selected with care using a range of different pen tools.*

Photoshop is image-editing software. Therefore its ability to create images from scratch, rather than modifying existing ones, is either limited or very cumbersome. You will find that Photoshop's capabilities will be most effective once your calligraphy has been created or captured, rather than as a means of helping you to write the calligraphy itself. This is because the software is bitmap-based and works on a pixel-by-pixel basis. Editing shapes, including letters, without the use of marks or filters is not really practical. The software has some vector working facilities but these in no way compare with those in specialized drawing programs such as Adobe Illustrator or CorelDraw. That is not to say that Photoshop can't be used to create the original calligraphy, but you will be challenged to find your own approach using its pen and brush tools to generate effective script. Once you recognize the potential of digital calligraphy you may well be encouraged to move on and purchase drawing software that will integrate well with Photoshop and permit you to expand your creative potential to the full.

The screenshots used throughout the book to indicate the use of menus, tools, palette options, and so on have been taken from Photoshop version 8.0, part of the Adobe Creative Suite and also known as Photoshop CS. There is little in this version compared with versions 6 or 7 that has any effect on what you can do with the software. The only new relevant addition is the ability to put text on a path and edit it like any other text. This function applies only to text input (i.e. fonts) and you cannot place or write your calligraphy on a path, unless, of course, you create a typeface from it. You should not be limited by using most of the earlier versions of Photoshop.

It is hoped that this book will identify procedures and methods that you haven't used before for lettering applications and will guide you to new ways of working with digital calligraphy.

C *Photoshop is most effective when used to modify images. Here some preset styles have been applied to calligraphic capitals.*

c

U ntil you become a proficient Photoshop user, you will probably initiate procedures and select options with the mouse via menus, icons, and so on. However, if you check your Photoshop manual (or the *Edit>**Keyboard Shortcuts*** menu) you will find keyboard shortcuts for all the selections and operations, which could save you time and effort in the long term.

The Photoshop default working screen resembles that of most advanced graphics programs with a *Menu bar*, *Tool Options bar*, *Toolbox*, the *Palette well*, and palettes. The *Tool Options bar* changes according to the tool

SOFTWARE

Tools, menus, option bars, and palettes

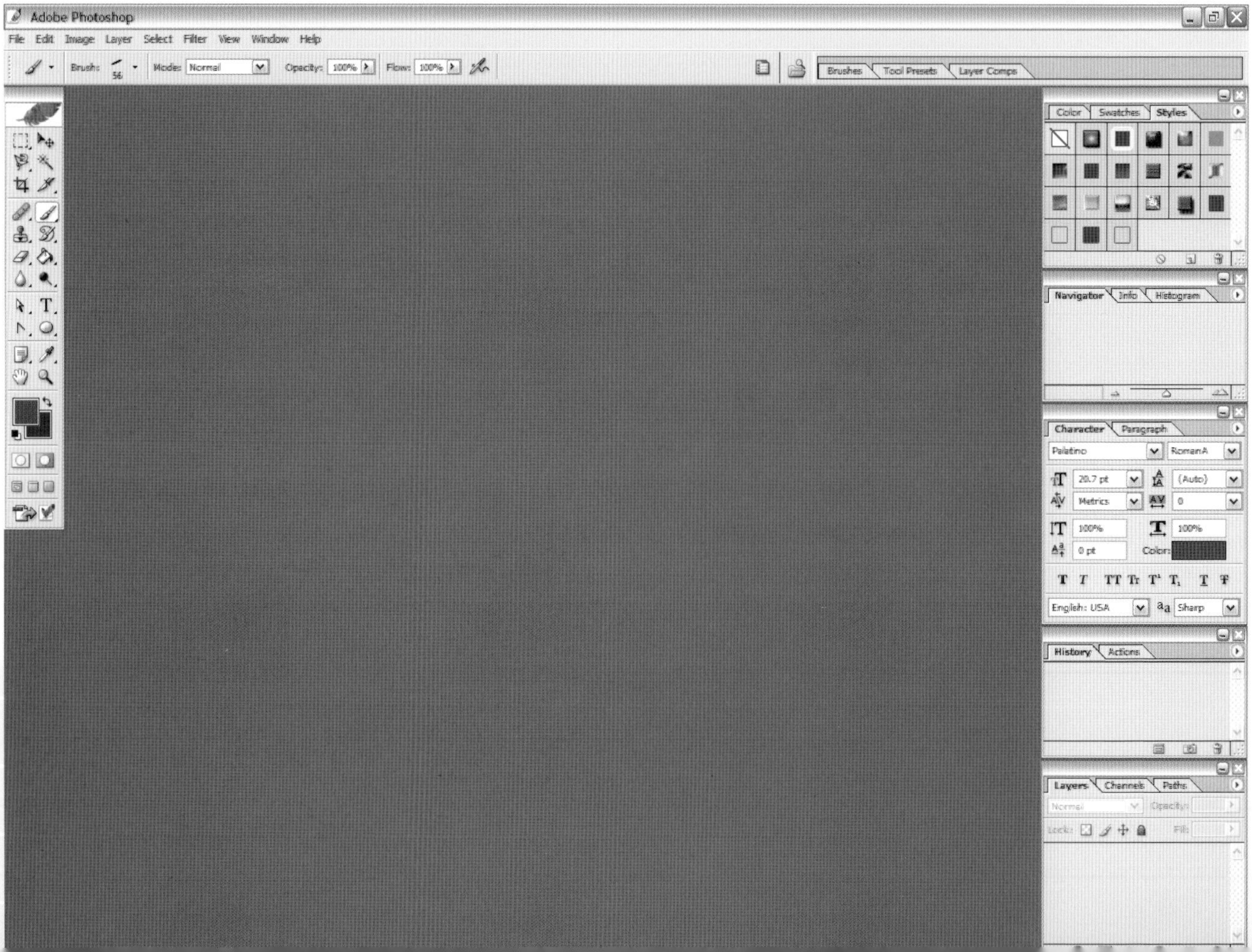

A

selected from the *Toolbox*. For example, if the *Brush* tool is selected, options are displayed for the *Tool preset picker*, the *Brush preset picker, Mode, Opacity,* and *Flow*. The *Palette well* includes drop-down palettes for *Brushes, Tool Presets,* and *Layer Comps*. The *Toolbox* and palettes are floating and can be dragged to anywhere on the screen. Note that the little button on the top right of the palettes brings up a new range of options. In the *Toolbox*, holding down the mouse button (left mouse button on the PC) on most of the tool icons opens a flyout with further tool selections (hidden tools). At first, Photoshop's work area looks rather daunting with so many options visible on screen. You can minimize palettes to make more of the work area visible. One of the main difficulties of learning to use complex applications is remembering where every

main menu item is located and what each one offers as options. It is very easy to miss things that could be very useful. Making notes can be helpful.

As is common with more powerful computer graphics software, the Photoshop work area can very easily become cluttered. There are ways of reducing the number of visible items on screen. One method is to dock the floating palettes to the docking well to maximize your work area on screen, provided you remember where they are. Always keep the *Layers/Channels/Paths* palette very close at hand as you will be accessing it regularly.

A *Photoshop's work area looks rather daunting until you become familiar with it.*

B *When a tool is selected from the Toolbox the Tool Options bar changes to display the specific options for that tool. Here those for the Brush tool have been displayed. The various options are usually available via drop-down menus.*

C *Each palette has its own subpalette that is accessed via the top tabs. You can access a further range of options and settings by clicking on the little button on the top right of the palette window. One of the options here is to dock the palette to the palette well. Note that there are icons along the bottom of the palette that, in this case, let you clear, create, or delete a style.*

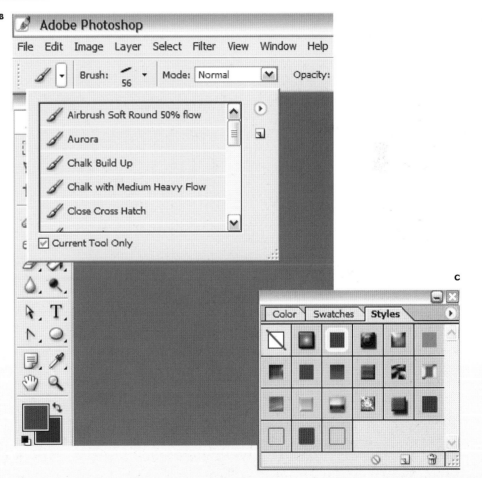

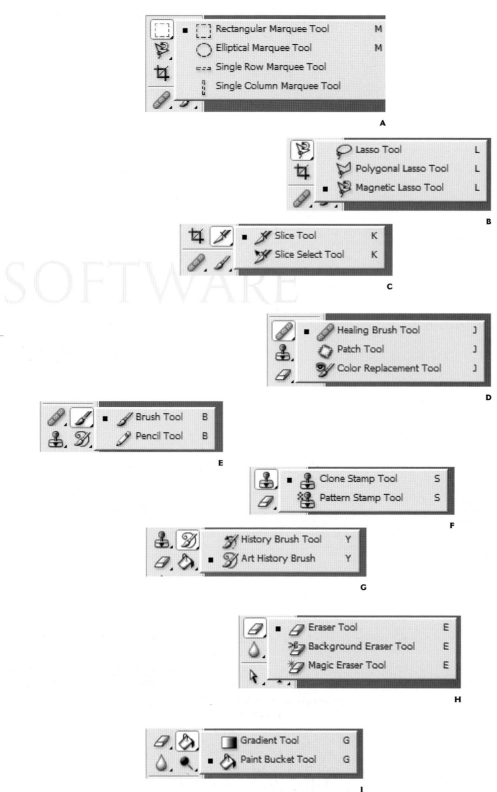

A The Marquee tool encloses a portion of an image with a marquee of the selected shape. Drag across the desired portion of the image.

B The Lasso tool selects a portion of an image by drawing around the shape. You will use the Magnetic Lasso tool to select the outline of individual letters.

C The Slice tool is used in the preparation of Web graphics to apply Web effects.

D The Healing Brush tool clones part of an image like the Clone Stamp tool but without obscuring the texture and shading of the original.

E The Brush tool is used for drawing and painting. We will use this a lot to create our calligraphy.

F The Clone Stamp tool paints one area of an image with graphics taken from another area.

G The History tool is a special type of undo brush that reverts portions of an image to a previous state.

H The Eraser tool lets you paint in the background colour or reveal layers below the current one.

I The Paint Bucket tool fills an area with a predefined colour or pattern. The Gradient tool creates a transition of colours by dragging it across an image.

SOFTWARE

J *The Blur, Sharpen, and Smudge tools let you soften or sharpen an image. Smudge enables you to literally smudge a digital image by pushing the pixels around.*

K *The Dodge, Burn, and Sponge tools let you lighten, darken, or decrease saturation of an image.*

L *The Selection tool lets you select the paths and segments of a vector shape, including vector calligraphy.*

M *The Type tool is used for entering text in the selected font, size, and orientation.*

N *The Pen tools let you draw and modify paths and add, delete, and convert anchor points.*

O *The Shape tool is used to draw predefined vector shapes and lines including rectangles, circles, ellipses, and user-defined polygons.*

P *With the Notes tool you can add a memo to your image or create an audio annotation.*

Q *The Eyedropper tool selects the foreground or background colour from a colour on screen.*

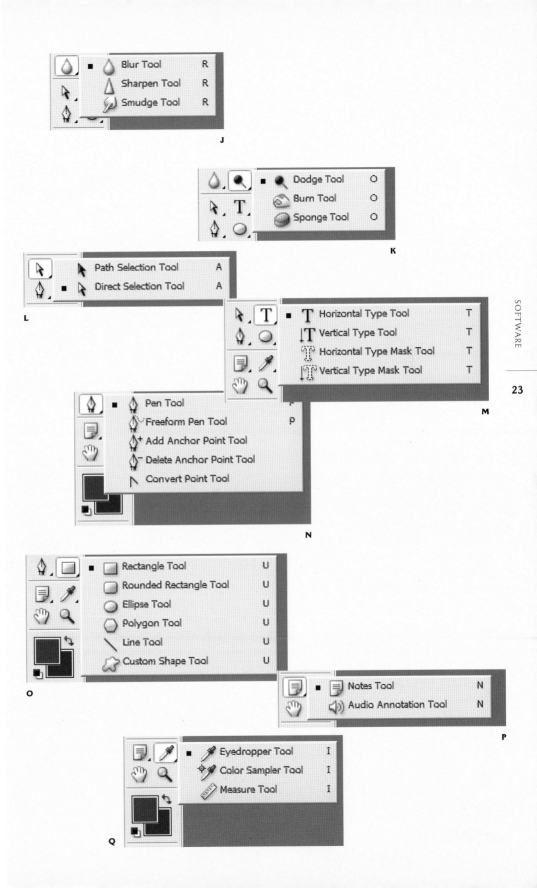

Blur Tool   R
Sharpen Tool   R
Smudge Tool   R

J

Dodge Tool   O
Burn Tool   O
Sponge Tool   O

K

Path Selection Tool   A
Direct Selection Tool   A

L

Horizontal Type Tool   T
Vertical Type Tool   T
Horizontal Type Mask Tool   T
Vertical Type Mask Tool   T

M

Pen Tool
Freeform Pen Tool   P
Add Anchor Point Tool
Delete Anchor Point Tool
Convert Point Tool

N

Rectangle Tool   U
Rounded Rectangle Tool   U
Ellipse Tool   U
Polygon Tool   U
Line Tool   U
Custom Shape Tool   U

O

Notes Tool   N
Audio Annotation Tool   N

P

Eyedropper Tool   I
Color Sampler Tool   I
Measure Tool   I

Q

Presets enable you to save settings for specific tools, keep a record of how you created a particular effect, and much more. As a simple example, you could save the precise setting for your calligraphic brush to avoid having to do this every time you want to use it. The *Preset Manager*, accessed through *Edit>***Preset Manager** from the menu bar or from the specific palette menu, helps you to organize and store your presets in eight different categories: *Brushes*, *Swatches*, *Gradients*, *Styles*, *Patterns*, *Contours*, *Custom Shapes*, and *Tools*.

SOFTWARE

Presets, colour, and undo

A

B

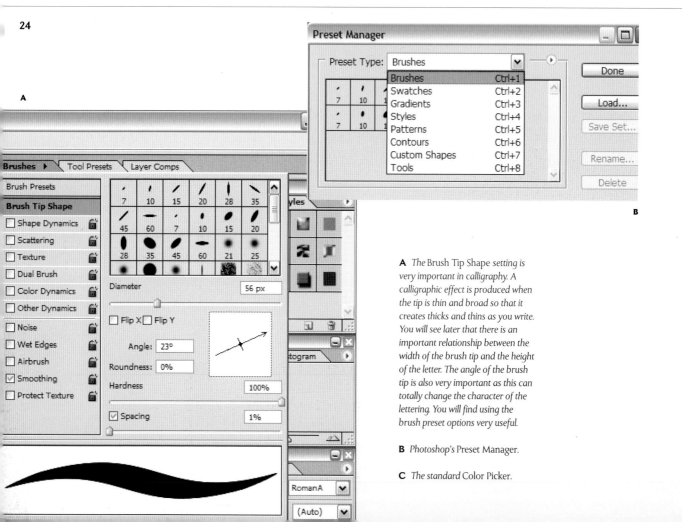

A *The* Brush Tip Shape *setting is very important in calligraphy. A calligraphic effect is produced when the tip is thin and broad so that it creates thicks and thins as you write. You will see later that there is an important relationship between the width of the brush tip and the height of the letter. The angle of the brush tip is also very important as this can totally change the character of the lettering. You will find using the brush preset options very useful.*

B *Photoshop's* Preset Manager.

C *The standard* Color Picker.

In digital calligraphy you will frequently change and set the foreground and background colours via the *Toolbox*. Single-clicking on either icon will display the *Color Picker*. This lets you select from the millions of colours that should be available on your computer system. Don't forget that there are many ways of changing colours in your design, so when you pick one you will not be finally committed to it.

Some of the most important options that you will find in Photoshop are *Undo*, *Step Backward*, and the *History* palette. All of these options allow you to recover from the mistakes that we all make. *Undo* simply reverts one step to the position that you were in before the last action. The *Step Backward* option does what it says and permits you to go back through a number of previous actions (the number is definable in Photoshop's *Preferences*). The *History* palette lets you go back more than one step at a time and to remove selected actions simultaneously. As Photoshop has to store all these temporary images, this is one of the reasons it is so demanding on computer resources.

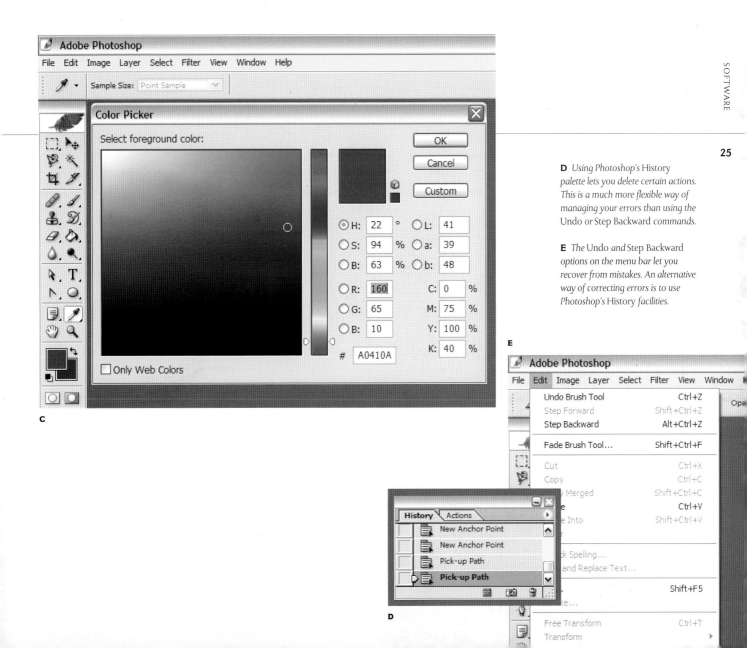

D *Using Photoshop's History palette lets you delete certain actions. This is a much more flexible way of managing your errors than using the* Undo *or* Step Backward *commands.*

E *The* Undo *and* Step Backward *options on the menu bar let you recover from mistakes. An alternative way of correcting errors is to use Photoshop's History facilities.*

If you can achieve effective calligraphic imagery using Photoshop without being too observant of the traditional values of good letterform, then so be it. It is certainly possible to enjoy artworks based on calligraphic marks that have little or nothing to do with what we accept as the letters of our alphabet. One of the qualities of great calligraphy, in the more generally accepted sense, is that it communicates the content of the text as well as adding expression through the ebb and flow of the pen. Arguably, legibility achieved through good letterform adds deeper meaning to the artwork.

An appreciation of good letterform contributes to the aesthetic pleasure that we can get from lettering written by skilled scribes.

We tend to think of letters as linear forms, especially when they are written with a pen. However, every letter has two facets, line and shape. Calligraphic letters are created from one or more pen strokes that define their basic forms. For example, the lowercase 'o' is a circle or ellipse, 'h' comprises a vertical stroke and an arching line, 's' is formed from a single wavy line, and 'x' is formed from two diagonals crossing each other. Straight lines need not

CALLIGRAPHY
The importance of good letterform

26

A *Letters are formed from linear strokes that define the basic forms.*

B *The counters of the letters are as important as the lines that define the form.*

C *The spaces created between letters in words are very important when determining the distance that each letter should be from its adjacent neighbor.*

D *In calligraphy the strokes that make up letters are rarely straight.*

be perfectly straight. Indeed, in calligraphy there is hardly ever a straight line. However, if the linear definition of the letter deviates too far from the basic form, the lettering is no longer legible. Our alphabet is a code and there is a limit to how far we can change the elements of the code before they are no longer understood by others.

Letters also have shape. This is defined by the stroke or strokes of the letter. The letter 'o', for example, encloses a circular or elliptical shape. This is called the 'counter'. Many letters have open counters. The lowercase 'm', for instance, has two open arch-shaped counters. A poorly shaped counter destroys the form of the letter. Letters create further shape when they are placed together in the form of words. These interletter shapes are extremely important in the adjustment of good

letter spacing. When we draw letters it is not difficult to assess how well formed we have made the stroke and counter shape. When we write with a pen, both aspects have to be controlled simultaneously.

An appreciation of good letterform is not acquired overnight but there are ways in which an understanding of the principles can be reinforced. You can learn a great deal by drawing and tracing typefaces, especially if this is done on a large scale. You will learn far more by actually recreating the forms, rather than just looking at them on a computer screen. Draw both the lines of the letters and the counter shapes, perhaps in different colours. Another good exercise is to trace calligraphy by writing it over an enlarged copy, using tracing or layout paper. By so doing you will see how the calligrapher formed the letters.

E *When is a 'd' not a 'd?' If part of a letter is altered so much that it changes its basic form, the letter is no longer legible.*

F *You can learn a lot from drawing typefaces. Draw both the linear and the counter parts of each letter.*

G *Use this example to copy the calligraphy to find out how each letter was formed. Make a photocopy first and work from that or you could damage your book!*

E

F

G

In practice, we should not be concerned with definitions and semantics, lettering designers and calligraphers will work with forms that are appropriate for the job in hand, whatever they are called.

If we accept the definition of calligraphy as 'beautiful writing' or 'writing as an art form' we can include anything that is based on written forms. Within this definition we could include calligraphy in which the text is no longer legible but retains the 'artistic' qualities that come from the skilled use of a writing instrument. Although there are several different viewpoints, most people recognize calligraphic letterform when it retains the characteristics of a broad-edged pen, creating distinctive thick and thin lines. In some contemporary calligraphy the broad-edged pen origins have been all but lost.

Edward Johnston, who laid the ground rules for much of the calligraphy of the twentieth century, included in his 'qualities of good calligraphy' what he called 'sharpness.' By this he meant that the letters should be true to the broad-edged pen. They should clearly show that, when the scribe was writing, the edge of the pen was held at a consistent angle. By so doing, the thick and thin parts of the letters would be in a logical and consistent place. He also emphasized the requirement for the thin strokes to contrast with the thick ones. When we come to use the Photoshop tools, calligraphic pen angle will be an

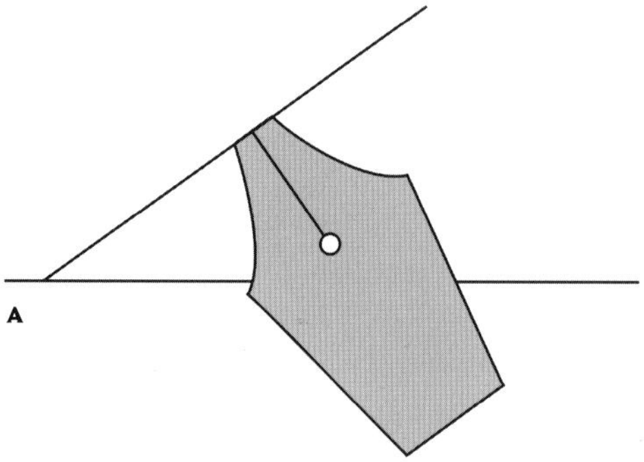

Calligraphic letterform

A

B

C

important consideration. Although the term 'pen angle' is being used here, in Photoshop's terms this means that the *Brush* tool is set to an appropriately calligraphic shape. Creating the difference between thick and thin strokes will be achieved by using tool presets and, as such, is not a matter of concern.

Changing the pen angle dramatically changes the characteristics of the letterform. The pen angle should never be obtuse (from top left to bottom right) as this will distort the form. Each calligraphic style requires the pen tip to be used within a particular angle range. The very round uncial form can be written with the pen tip almost horizontal. The 'foundation', 'round', or 'roman' hand is written with an angle of about 30 to 35 degrees, while the angle can be increased to as much as 45 degrees for italic.

The relationship between the pen tip width and the letter height is another very important consideration. If the width of the tip is too great, it can be difficult to construct some letters satisfactorily. On the other hand, if the nib is too narrow, the letters can look spindly and the pen stroke can be difficult to control.

There is little point in retaining good letterform if it is then destroyed by adding excessively complex flourishes or any other appendage that doesn't 'grow' for the basic letter. Be careful when you extend an ascender or descender or when you modify a serif. Be extra careful when you add a calligraphic flourish. When it is so easy to write flowing lines on the computer screen there is a great temptation to overuse the technique. If you wish to retain good letterform, be restrained.

A *The broad-edged pen should be kept at a constant angle to the writing line. When you come to write in Photoshop with calligraphic brushes, the same principle applies.*

B *The same letter written with different pen angles. From left to right: 45 degrees, 30 degrees, horizontal, and minus 30 degrees. This illustrates why the pen angle should not be obtuse.*

C *Different calligraphic lettering styles are written with the broad edge of the pen held at different angles. The uncial is written with an angle of zero to 5 degrees, roman (foundation) at about 30 degrees, and italic at an angle of between 40 and 45 degrees.*

D *Keeping the pen angle constant ensures that the thick and thin parts of calligraphic strokes will be in the correct relative place.*

D

A

A calligrapher's vocabulary

Calligraphers, lettering designers, and typographers use some terms that are specific to their discipline. You will find these terms used throughout this book.

30

B

A These are some of the terms used to refer to different parts of letters.

B A well-formed branching stroke of a letter in calligraphy, especially in an italic script, ensures good letterform and contributes to the rhythmic quality of the writing.

C The height of the capital in calligraphy should be less than the height of the ascender so that it doesn't appear too light in weight.

D The traditional calligraphic writing instrument is the broad-edged pen, where 'edge' refers to the width of the nib.

E The weight of letters in calligraphy is determined by the pen width and letter height.

C

ASCENDER AND DESCENDER
The parts of the lower case letters that rise above (as in 'b', 'd', 'h', 'k', and 'l') and below (as in 'g', 'j', 'p', and 'y') the x-height.

BASELINE
The bottom line of the x-height.

BODY
The overall height of a letter, that is the x-height plus the ascender and the descender.

BOWL
The closed curve of some letters such as 'b', 'd', 'p', and 'q'.

BRANCHING STROKE
An arching stroke that arises from a down stroke of a letter.

BROAD-EDGED PEN
A pen with a writing tip that has a chisel-shaped end, sometimes called a square-edged pen.

CAP OR CAPITAL HEIGHT
The height from the baseline to the top of the capital letters.

CAPS OR CAPITALS
The initial or 'large' letters of an alphabet.

CONDENSED
A narrow version of an alphabet or font.

COUNTER
The space contained within the round parts of some letters.

CURSIVE
In the lettering sense, scriptlike, or flowing.

EXPANDED
A wide version of an alphabet or font.

FLOURISH
An (nonessential) embellishment added to a letter.

FOUNDATION OR ROUND HAND
A simple roman calligraphic style. In its simplest form used to teach the basic skills of calligraphy.

HAND
The writing style of a calligrapher.

ITALIC
A script form developed in the Renaissance. Also a slanting version of a typeface, sometimes of a slightly different and more cursive style.

LEGIBILITY
At its simplest, how well text can be read. A complex concept that includes readability, visibility, and comprehension.

LETTER SPACING
The white space between letters. This is different from the physical distance between letters.

LIGHT, MEDIUM, AND BOLD (WEIGHT)
Letter styles that are thin, medium, or heavy in visual weight when compared with each other.

LINE OR INTERLINE SPACE
The space that lies between lines of text.

LOWERCASE (LETTERS)
The small letters of an alphabet or font, as opposed to capitals.

NIB WIDTH
The width of the writing end of a broad-edged pen.

pen width

D

PAPYRUS
A grass grown in the eastern Mediterranean that was woven into flat sheets and used by the ancient Egyptians and other early cultures as a writing surface.

PARCHMENT
A writing material made from animal skin, including calf (as vellum), sheep, and goat.

PEN ANGLE
The angle the writing tip of the broad-edged pen makes with the horizontal writing line.

ROMAN
The upright version of a typeface or alphabet. In the strict sense, forms with serifs.

SERIF
The short, sharp strokes at the end of a letter's main strokes.

STYLE
The character of a letterform. Style can be a general term or can refer more specifically to such variants as roman, italic, condensed, etc.

THICK (STROKE)
The broad line produced when writing with a broad-edged pen.

THIN (STROKE)
The thin line produced when writing with a broad-edged pen.

UNCIAL
An early form of writing that lacks capitals and that was developed from the Roman scripts.

WEIGHT
The relative darkness of the characters in an alphabet or script.

X-HEIGHT
The height of the lowercase letter 'x'.

*The traditional writing tool of the scribe is the
from the wing feather of a goose or other bird.
(the part that attached it to the bird) is trimr
square or chisel-shaped tip. This is usually re
The important characteristic of the broad-edg
thin strokes and produces the famil*

The traditional writing tool of the scribe is the
from the wing feather of a goose or other bird.
(the part that attached it to the bird) is trimr
square or chisel-shaped tip. This is usually re
The important characteristic of the broad-edg
thin strokes and produces the famil

E

The traditional writing equipment of a calligrapher is the pen, ink, and a writing surface. From the Dark Ages until well into the nineteenth century most scribes used a quill pen. This was made by cutting the end of the feather, the part that would have been attached to the bird, usually a goose, to a chisel-shaped tip – the broad-edged pen. The medieval scribes removed most of the veins from the feather: if they did not, the pen would be badly balanced. If you think about it, it would not be very practical to have the feather tickling your ear when you write – don't believe the movie producers! Today most calligraphers use metal pens that are of exactly the same shape as the natural instrument. These come in a range of sizes, from 00 (the largest) to 6, although anything smaller than 4½ is of little practical use for calligraphy. Penholders are a matter of calligraphers' preference.

Good calligraphic ink is made from a carbon compound and is not waterproof. Waterproof inks have a resin base that can make it difficult to get a good contrast between the thick and thin strokes of the lettering and can also clog the pen. If the work is to be permanent and vibrant colours are wanted, then artists'

Traditional approaches: materials and methods

A

B

A *Medieval Gothic script on vellum from a fourteenth-century psalter.*

B *Contrary to the popular belief, most of the veins of a feather were removed to make a usable pen.*

C *The ascender, x-height, and descender can be measured by using the pen tip vertically to form short strokes.*

D *Different formal calligraphic styles are written with different pen width to letter height ratios.*

watercolour is best, mixed with a little water to make it run through the pen. A little gum can be added to replace the lost binding medium.

When papyrus ceased to be the principal writing surface, manuscripts were written on vellum or parchment made from animal skin. Even today, vellum is preferred by a few calligraphers for very important work. From the sixteenth century onward paper was used increasingly and is now the most widely accepted material. For lettering that is to be scanned and transferred to the computer for use in Photoshop, black ink on a smooth, white surface (e.g. layout paper) is a good choice.

The calligraphic pen is filled with a brush from below, not dipped. If letters are to be of 'normal' proportions the height of the letter is determined by a number of pen nib widths. These vary according to the form to be written – the fewer nib widths to make up the letter height, the bolder or darker the letters will be. The uncial should have an x-height of about 4 to 4½ widths, the roman or foundation hand, about 4½ widths, and the italic about 5. The ascenders and descenders have to be proportionally longer for the lighter-weight styles. For formal calligraphy, accurate ruling of guidelines in pencil is extremely important. However, for free calligraphy these are often unnecessary.

Most of the above describes traditional equipment, but anything that will make a mark on a surface can be used as a calligraphy pen. Felt-tipped pens with broad tips are available. Pencils with large diameter leads can be trimmed to a square edge. For large work, paintbrushes or chalk held on its edge can simulate the calligraphic pen.

c

uncial
foundation
italic

D

Whether you produce your calligraphy by the traditional methods or in Photoshop, some of the basic principles are the same. We have already discussed the importance of letterform and of line and shape. When letters are assembled together in words, sentences, paragraphs, or pages the overall visual impression becomes central. No matter how well the individual letters are formed, they must come together satisfactorily as a design. Layout will be covered elsewhere in the book. Here we are concerned with the appearance of the calligraphy itself and the visual aspects of rhythm, pattern, and texture.

Calligraphy should be intrinsically rhythmic. Usually the rhythm of the lettering arises from the act of writing, rather than drawing the script. Some very formal styles, such as uncials and more formal romans, are more constructed than written, being formed from a series of discrete pen strokes. However, even these have a visual rhythm that is due to the repetition of very similar pen strokes. In the case of a foundation hand, for example, the pen strokes that form the verticals of the lowercase 'a', 'i', 'm', 'n', 'r', and 'u' are the same, as are the long verticals of 'b', 'd', 'h', 'k', and 'l'. Similarly, the curves on the left side of

Rhythm, pattern, and visual texture

imnr

bdhkl

acego

A

B

'a' are the same as those on the left side of 'c', 'e', 'g', and 'o'. This rhythm is more obvious in italic where it is emphasized by the verticals, the 'arching' in letters such as 'a', 'n', and 'm' and the natural linking of letter groups. From this it will be clear that keeping the angles of these lines as constant as possible is critical if a good rhythmic effect is to be achieved.

Pattern is determined by the scale of the lettering, the rhythmic writing of the script, and how this relates to interline spacing. Large, tightly spaced calligraphy will create quite a different visual pattern from small writing that has each line well separated.

Visual texture is easy to recognize but difficult to describe. Some calligraphy looks rich and 'busy', while some is very 'quiet' and restrained. These are rather romantic notions, but it is visual texture that creates the initial impression when we look at a piece of calligraphic work. It is the cumulative effect of rhythm and pattern and gives the calligraphy its 'feel'. The slightest consistent change in the form of a serif, an ascender or a descender can have a very dramatic effect on the visual texture of a block of text. We can see this clearly in typefaces that appear to differ little when we study their basic individual forms but that create quite different effects when set in a paragraph.

The use of contrasting rhythm, pattern, and visual texture, together with changes in scale and colour, can be used to great effect in calligraphic design.

There are many good books that describe traditional calligraphic techniques. Here we have given some principles and guidance to get you started.

HAVING ACQUIRED A FORMAL HAND THE PENMAN MAY MODIFY AND ALTER IT, TAKING CARE THAT THE CHANGES ARE COMPATIBLE, AND THAT THEY DO NOT IMPAIR ITS LEGIBILITY OR BEAUTY. SUCH LETTERS AS ARE OBSOLETE HE REPLACES BY LEGIBLE FORMS AKIN TO THEM IN FEELING, AND, THE STYLE OF THE SELECTED TYPE BECOMING VERY NATURALLY AND ALMOST UNCONSCIENTIOUSLY MODIFIED BY PERSONAL USE, HE AT LENGTH ATTAINS AN APPROPRIATE AND MODERN FORMAL-HANDWRITING. THE PROCESS OF 'FORMING' A HAND REQUIRES TIME AND PRACTICE: IT RESEMBLES THE PASSAGE OF 'COPY-BOOK' INTO 'RUNNING' HAND, FAMILIAR TO US ALL.

Having acquired a formal hand the penman may modify and alter it, taking care that the changes are compatible, and that they do not impair its legibility or beauty. Such letters as are obsolete he replaces by legible forms akin to them in feeling, and, the style of the selected type becoming very naturally and almost unconscientiously modified by personal use, he at length attains an appropriate and modern Formal-Handwriting. The process of 'forming' a hand requires time and practice; it resembles the passage of 'Copy-book' into 'Running' hand, familiar to us all.

C

Having acquired a formal hand the penman may modify and alter it, taking care that the changes are compatible, and that they do not impair its legibility or beauty. Such letters as are obsolete he replaces by legible forms akin to them in feeling, and, the style of the selected type becoming very naturally and almost unconscientiously modified by personal use, he at length attains an appropriate and modern Formal-Handwriting. The process of 'forming' a hand requires time and practice: it resembles the passage of 'Copy-book' into 'Running' hand, familiar to us all.

Having acquired a formal hand the penman may modify and alter it, taking care that the changes are compatible, and that they do not impair its legibility or beauty. Such letters as are obsolete he replaces by legible forms akin to them in feeling, and, the style of the selected type becoming very naturally and almost unconscientiously modified by personal use, he at length attains an appropriate and modern Formal-Handwriting. The process of 'forming' a hand requires time and practice: it resembles the passage of 'Copy-book' into 'Running' hand, familiar to us all.

D

A Calligraphic letters are formed by writing the same pen strokes repeatedly with only slight variations. Attention to this helps to develop a rhythm in the writing.

B Calligraphy, especially italic, has a rhythm that is due to parts of the letters and their joins being formed from a series of parallel lines.

C Textual pattern changes with both letterform and line spacing, as here with an uncial and an italic.

D Visual texture is easy to recognize but hard to define. Here two similar italic forms form blocks of text with very different textures.

STARTING A PROJECT

Image size and resolution

A Set the basic parameters of your image by using the command File>**New** and then setting the width, height, and resolution. Note that your file size increases with the canvas size and resolution.

B Zooming into an image reveals pixelation but doesn't alter the actual image. Don't confuse zoom with resolution.

C This illustration demonstrates the effect of increasing the image resolution: left to right 75, 150, and 300 pixels per inch.

D The image size can be changed even after you have been working on the calligraphy. You can change width, height, and resolution. Use this rather than resizing if you want to retain the quality of your work.

E Drag the Crop tool over the image to select the area that you want to retain.

F Click within the selected area and your document will be resized.

B

C

If you are familiar with the basics of using graphics software you will already know how to set up the screen for your particular project. Different software applications have slight differences in the way image size, canvas size, and resolution are selected. In all cases, the menu items are relatively easy to find and use. Image size and resolution are interrelated and should not be confused with the actual size of the image that you see on screen. This is determined by the zoom factor. If you compare different image sizes and resolutions on screen you must do so at the same zoom level, for example at 100%.

Image size and resolution, together with colour depth, will determine the ultimate quality of your creation, if this is assessed by the sharpness and total colour range. Increasing the quality comes at a price. Each of these factors will increase file size and also the speed with which the more resource-hungry Photoshop operations will be performed.

When you start a project, decide how your finished work will be displayed. Will it exist as 'virtual' calligraphy, to be seen only on a computer screen of 17 or 21 inches across? Will it be printed on a simple A4 colour inkjet printer? Or will it be printed on a large-format, high-quality inkjet printer on a much larger scale? Decide on the final or optimum desired size and proportion of your calligraphic design, and set the width and height (*File*>**New** – then enter the sizes in the pop-up window).

Whether you use inches, centimetres, pixels, or one of the other units is entirely up to you but it is best to use the same system for both height and width. This is your 'canvas size'. The canvas can be resized but remember that if you enlarge the canvas, the number of pixels remains the same and the visual effect is similar to zooming. On the other hand, if you resample the image you can adjust the number of pixels and retain sharpness and quality.

If you work to a 'same size' image, it is much easier to determine the resolution. Calligraphy is usually, though not always, 'hard edge' and you will want your lettering to be as sharp as possible. This means you should use a fairly high resolution (set in the same window as height and width), perhaps as high as 200 or 300 pixels to the inch. If your work doesn't include 'hard-edge' lettering you can use a lower setting. Note that in Photoshop you can change the resolution of your image later, even after the design is complete. If some of your calligraphy will be very small in size you will need a higher resolution.

When you are working on your design, or when it is finished, you may want to crop it and remove unwanted parts at the margins. Photoshop provides several methods of cropping an image. The chances are that you will want to make a simple rectangular crop. The easiest way to do this is to select the *Crop* tool, drag it across the image to the desired size and proportion, and click the mouse button.

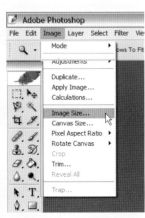

If you have colour facilities – a colour monitor and a colour printer – you will probably want to use colour in your calligraphy. Sometimes, however, you will want to work in monochrome (greyscale or line art), possibly for a small item like an invitation or card that will simply be printed on a laser printer or photocopied. If that is the case you should set your colour mode to greyscale so that your file size is small and your computer will run faster.

In Photoshop you are offered five colour modes: *Bitmap*, *Grayscale*, *RGB*, *CMYK*, and *Lab*. When you work with photographic images on your computer it is important that the colour is faithful to the original subject. Unwanted colour casts, especially on flesh colours, are distracting and quite unacceptable. Abstract imagery, and this includes calligraphy, does not present these problems. Even to those of us with the most acute colour perception, a relatively simple colour spectrum is perfectly adequate.

There are several reasons why you should select the RGB colour mode. Red, green, and blue are the colour primaries of light, each having 256 levels of intensity or brightness. The more that each primary is added, the lighter the colour becomes – hence the term 'additive

STARTING A PROJECT

Colour formats

38

A *After using the command Window>****Color****, select the foreground and background colours from the Color palette, using the sliders to make fine adjustments.*

B *The additive colour primaries of red, green, and blue don't make the same colours as paint when mixed. Red and green make yellow, red and blue make magenta, green and blue make cyan, and all three combined will make white.*

C *The Channels palette, showing the three separate RGB channels, and one composite.*

primary model'. Add the full amount of each primary and you get white light. Reduce each to zero and you get black. Each of the three RGB primaries can be independently adjusted through Photoshop's *Channels*, thus providing a great level of control over the colour of the image. Almost all of Photoshop's file formats support RGB, the exceptions being GIF (which could be important if your calligraphy is to be used as, or part of, an image on the Web) and DCS. Only greyscale images can be saved in a wider range of file formats. Unfortunately, colour printing cannot cope with the same range of colours as the RGB colour model. To see the possible differences between what you see on screen and what will be output from your colour printer you should convert your RGB image into CMYK. It can then be edited in that mode, if necessary, although you will have access to a more limited colour spectrum. There are many advanced methods of editing available that can be used when preparing your images for print, but these are beyond the scope of this book. However, colours in calligraphy are rarely so critical that this will be a major hindrance.

Decide on your initial foreground and background colours. You can select them by clicking on the icons at the bottom of the *Toolbox* or from the *Color* palette. This second method lets you use sliders to select and adjust colours. By default, the RGB colour sliders will be displayed but these can be changed through the palette menu.

D *A simple way to set up the initial foreground and background colours is to select them from the Toolbox.*

E *You can change the colour mode from the palette options.*

F *Printing cannot reproduce all the colours that you will have available in the RGB palette (right). However, conversion of calligraphic work to CMYK (left) will rarely have a significant effect on the final print colours. (This effect is simulated.)*

You will be unlikely to ever use the majority of file formats that Photoshop can open and save to. The most common formats that you will come across are PSD, JPEG, and TIFF.

Firstly, let us consider Photoshop's own native format, which has the file extension PSD. While your work is in progress you should save it in this format as it will retain the full range of Photoshop features including layers, extra channels, file information etc. Why then should we ever consider saving in any other formats? If you have limitless disk storage space and have no intention of ever exporting the file to another program or don't plan to share your cherished work of art with anyone else, then there is no need to save it in another file format. Almost all file formats have their advantages and disadvantages. We have already seen that some colour modes, such as CMYK, use a limited colour range to match output devices, especially printers. Similarly, some file formats can work only in a reduced number of colours. This includes GIF which works in only 256 colours and is suited to Web applications. Here we will discuss two of the most widely used formats, TIFF (tif) and JPEG (jpg).

STARTING A PRO

File formats

40

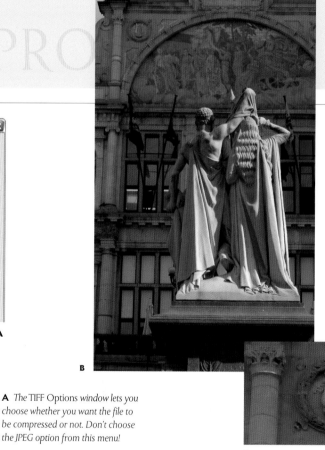

A The TIFF Options *window lets you choose whether you want the file to be compressed or not. Don't choose the JPEG option from this menu!*

B *This photograph of a monumental sculpture in Bruges, Belgium, was saved in TIFF format without compression. The image size is 38.7MB.*

C *A detail of the same image saved in TIFF format without compression. The file size is 293KB.*

Both TIFF and JPEG formats are highly portable and can be opened in most graphics programs. Occasionally, you can run into compatibility problems with TIFF files, as it has so many variants, although this situation is rare. Although not exclusive to TIFF and JPEG, they both have the great advantage that files saved in these formats can be compressed so that the file sizes are greatly reduced. They use very different compression methods, which have important effects on the image. JPEG compression works by discarding some digital information from the image. It is usually referred to as a 'lossy' method. The degree of degradation of the image depends on the degree of compression. JPEG files can be a tiny percentage of the full, uncompressed file. TIFF files, on the other hand, use a totally different method called LZW. This is not a lossy method and the full quality of your work is retained. However, it cannot compress the image to the same extent as JPEG. In reality, JPEG files have to be compressed significantly before there is a really noticeable loss of quality. Repeated saving of JPEG files progressively degrades the image, although in Photoshop you will reach a limit. Incidentally, never use the TIFF-JPEG option, as very few programs will be able to decode your file.

An important consideration in the case of calligraphic work is to what extent you want to retain the clean, sharp quality of the calligraphy. If this is important, as will almost always be the case, JPEG compression should be used with caution and TIFF with LZW compression is a far better option. If you need information on other file formats check the Photoshop manual or the *Help* menu.

D

E

F

G

D *The same photograph saved with LZW compression reduced the file to 20MB with no change in image quality.*

E *The detail saved in TIFF format with LZW compression. The file size is 149KB.*

F *Saving the image in JPEG format with maximum compression has reduced the file size to only 337KB, less than one percent of the original. The loss in quality at this scale is only just noticeable.*

G *A detail of the same image saved in JPEG format with maximum compression. The file size is only 17.4KB but the quality loss is considerable, in terms of both definition and colour.*

Step-by-step exercise: image resolution

42

1 Start a new document (File>**New**) and set the image size to 10 inches by 10 inches, and a resolution of 70 pixels per inch. Although we will be working in black and white, set the colour to RGB. Leave the Background Contents set to white.

2 In the Toolbox, ensure that the foreground colour is set to black and the background colour to white.

3 As we haven't yet covered creating calligraphy within Photoshop, we will use a calligraphic, script, or italic typeface. The example illustrated is Vivaldi. If you already know how to use the calligraphic brush, you can use that instead. With the Horizontal Type tool and a type size of 200 point, type two words in two lines (i.e. use your keyboard Return key between words).

4 Using the Move tool, drag the text until it is centred on your canvas.

5 Use the Zoom tool to zoom to 300%. You will see that the edges of the letters are very rough (pixelated). This is because we set the resolution to 70 pixels/inch. Zoom back to 100%.

6 With the command Image>**Image Size** in the **Image Size** window, change the resolution to 300 pixels/inch. As your apparent image size will have increased greatly you will have to pan the image to find your lettering.

3

5

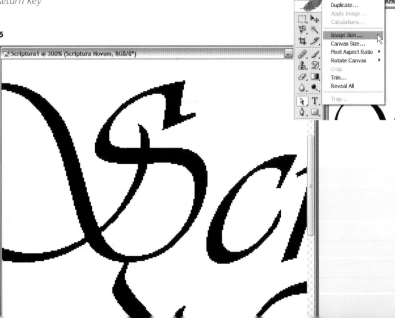

6

7 *Once again, zoom in to 300% and see the difference. Now the edges of the lettering are much smoother. Return to the original resolution of 70 pixels per inch using* Image>**Image Size**.

8 *From the drop-down menus select* Layer>Rasterize>**Type**. *What we have done is, in effect, to convert the type to a true bitmap. As it is now an image, you will no longer be able to edit it as text.*

9 *Using* Image>**Image Size**, *increase the resolution again to 300 pixels/inch. You will see that this time the edges of the lettering have retained their roughness. We will use this as a special effect.*

10 *Zoom out so that you can see the whole canvas (fit to screen). With the* Horizontal Type *tool type the alphabet in three or four lines using a point size of 72 and leading of 30 points. This will cause the lines to overlap slightly and create a pattern. At this point you may wish to zoom into the lettering you have just typed to check that the edges are smooth.*

11 *Drag the text between the two words and to the right. If you zoom in you will see the nice contrast between the rough and script lettering.*

12 *To complete the design, type a large letter in 500 point and position it over the other lettering. The design may be a bit confusing, so we will change the tone of the large letter to gray. Ensure that the large letter layer is below the others. If it is not, drag it into position in the* Layers *palette.*

It was probably the poet John Milton in the middle of the seventeenth century who first used the term 'calligraphy' but it was not widely used until the nineteenth century. Calligraphy is 'beautiful writing' or 'writing as an art'. Although the labels are different now, calligraphy can be traced back to the days of the Pharoes in their papyrus manuscripts written in scripts called hieratic and demotic. These were written with a pen cut to a broad, chisel shaped tip, creating thick and thick strokes. The Romans also wrote with a reed pen cut in a similar way and their rustic capitals show how the writing instrument affected the form of the letters.

STARTING A PROJECT

Step-by-step exercise: working with colour

1 In this exercise we will use the same image size as in the previous example (10 inches by 10 inches) and use a script or calligraphic typeface or Photoshop calligraphy if you wish. The typeface used in the example is Lucida Calligraphy. Start a new document and set the parameters.

2 Set the foreground colour to black and the background to white. Set the text size to 120 point, the leading to 70, the alignment to centred and type the alphabet in capitals or lowercase, three letters at a time with a return in between. You will have only two letters in the last line. The letters of each line should overlap slightly. Use the Move tool to centre the lettering.

3 Select the lettering with the Horizontal Type tool and change the colour to one of your choice using the icon at the bottom of the Toolbox.

4 Using the Magic Wand tool, select some of the counter shapes in the design. Hold down the Shift key so that multiple areas can be selected. Try to create a balance of the selections.

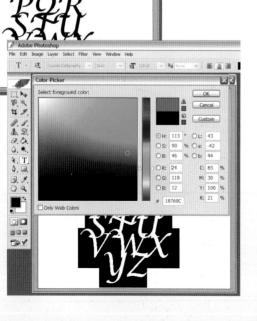

2

3

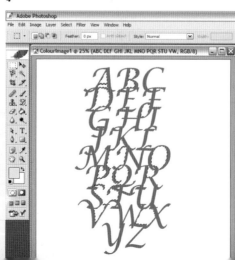

4

5

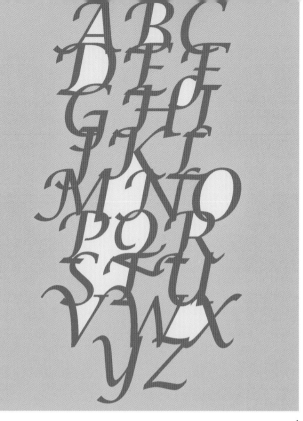

6

5 *Change the foreground colour to one that goes well with the colour of the lettering. Using the* Paint Bucket *tool click within one of the selected counters. The colour will now fill all of the counters, even if they are not physically linked. Remove the mask.*

6 *Now choose another foreground colour. With the* Paint Bucket *tool fill the background of your design. Note that the whole white area is filled and is not interrupted by the other colours.*

7 *The colour we have chosen may not work too well. In our example, change the hue of the orange and make it a bit more vibrant and interesting. For this we will adjust one of the colour channels. In the* Channels *palette select green. Your design will change to greyscale. Don't worry – you are seeing the green element of the RGB colour mode.*

8 *From the main drop-down menus select* Image> Adjustments>**Levels**. *This will display a window in which you can change the amount of green (or one of the other channels that you have selected). Ensure that Preview is checked. Moving the sliders (three for input levels and three for output levels) will lighten or darken the grey tone of your image and consequently adjust the amount of green in the layer of the image. You will also see that the little RGB icon in the* Channels *palette also changes as you adjust the levels. We will explore other ways of adjusting colour later.*

9 *Type in two columns of centred text at about 14 point. Use some text from this book if you can't think of anything yourself. Locate the columns to either side of the original lettering. At this point you may wish to crop the image to complete the design.*

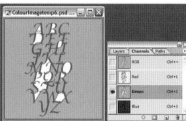

7

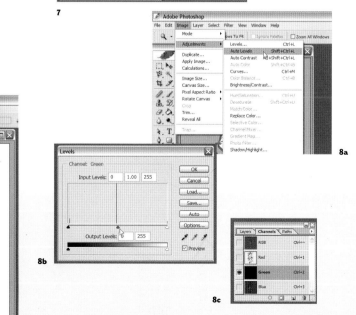

It was probably the poet John Milton in the middle of the seventeenth century who first used the term 'calligraphy' but it was not widely used until the nineteenth century. Calligraphy is 'beautiful writing' or 'writing as an art'. Although the labels are different now, calligraphy can be traced back to the days of

the Pharoes in their papyrus manuscripts written in scripts called hieratic and demotic. These were written with a pen cut to a broad, chisel shaped tip, creating thick and thick strokes. The Romans also wrote with a reed pen cut in a similar way and their rustic capitals show how the writing instrument affected the form of the letters.

8a

8b

8c

9

Ce que n'est pas bon pour soi,
N'est pas bon pour les autres,

CALLIGRAPHY ON SCREEN

Transferring calligraphy to the computer

B

Adobe Photoshop

File Edit Image Layer Select Filter View Window Help

New...   Ctrl+N
Open...   Ctrl+O
Browse...   Shift+Ctrl+O
Open As...   Alt+Ctrl+O
Open Recent

Edit in ImageReady   Shift+Ctrl+M

Close   Ctrl+W
Close All   Alt+Ctrl+W
Save   Ctrl+S
Save As...   Shift+Ctrl+S
Save a Version...
Save for Web...   Alt+Shift+Ctrl+S
Revert   F12

Place...

Online Services...

Import
Export

Automate
Scripts

PDF Image...
Annotations...
WIA Support...

e que n'est pas bon pou
'est pas bon pour les autres,

C

Ce que n'est pas bon pour soi,
N'est pas bon pour les autres,

D

A Original simple calligraphy written in black ink on white paper ready for scanning.

B Selecting File>**Import** will display the WIA (Windows Image Acquisition) option, which gives you access to digital camera and WIA compliant scanners. The more common Twain option will appear if your scanner is Twain compliant, giving you access to your own particular scanner software.

C Calligraphy scanned at 1000dpi for maximum quality.

D Calligraphy scanned at 300dpi. There is little loss of quality in this example but it may matter for some applications. The very slight texturing on the letters could be desirable.

E Calligraphy scanned at only 50dpi. Low-resolution scans of this quality are not really acceptable.

F Scanning small-scale writing can create some interesting effects when enlarged. Here the rough texture of the paper has affected the letterforms.

Photoshop's built-in tools are not much use for creating large amounts of formal calligraphic text. Having read that, perhaps you may want to close this book and go no further. But stop! We *can* use Photoshop as an extremely useful calligraphic tool in many other ways.

Calligraphy need not comprise paragraphs of continuous text. Some very effective calligraphic examples use only a few words. Company logos are often calligraphic and have frequently been created in Photoshop or a similar graphics program. Calligraphy need not be the formal, regular writing that highly skilled scribes can create but can be free and expressive deriving its vitality from the spontaneity of the writing tool – perhaps Photoshop's calligraphic brush. Where Photoshop really scores is as a tool for the development of creative visual ideas through multifarious graphic techniques and effects, many of which are easily achieved by the novice, yet can be taken to new heights by the expert. If we do not want to use the limited calligraphic writing techniques within Photoshop for all or part of a piece of calligraphy, there is an easy solution to the problem. By scanning calligraphy written on paper we can import the script and access a whole spectrum of tools and effects.

Even if you plan to use soft effects or in some way texturize your calligraphy, it is always best to start with lettering that is sharp. That means scanning it at a high resolution. Although you can scan colour work, unless you have already created some colour effects that you want to use, there is no need to use anything other than black ink. Scanning itself can be used creatively. For example, some interesting effects can be created by scanning very small writing at a high resolution. When this is enlarged in Photoshop, the texture of the writing surface is greatly exaggerated. Importing multiple scans can also be used creatively.

For calligraphy that you plan to import into Photoshop, the absolute minimum resolution that you should set your scanner to is 600 dots per inch (dpi), although something in excess of 1000dpi is preferable. Your scanning software will give you the choice to scan in colour, greyscale, or line (solid black and white). It might seem obvious that you should scan your calligraphy in simple black and white. It is much better, however, to scan the lettering greyscale and make any changes, if necessary, later. In Photoshop you will be able to adjust contrast and, if you want, convert the calligraphy to line. The chances are that you will be restricted to A4 by your scanner. This is all the more reason why you should scan at a very high resolution. Of course you can scan your work in small pieces and reassemble them in Photoshop. Save your files as TIFFs.

File sizes of high-resolution greyscale images can be large but the utilization of your disk space by the large files may be only temporary once the calligraphy is incorporated into the final piece and it is cropped, resampled, or saved in a compressed file format.

E

Ce que n'est pas bon pour soi,

N'est pas bon p

F

Ce que n'est pas bon pour so

N'est pas bon pour les autre

This very simple example demonstrates how scanned calligraphy can be used in Photoshop. We will use the calligraphy scanned for the illustration on the preceding pages, together with a scanned large letter 'B'. For use in this exercise, prepare two or three lines of calligraphy and a single large letter using black ink on paper. Don't be too concerned about your calligraphic skills at this stage. You don't even need to use a broad-edged calligraphic pen in this instance. The aim of the step-by-step example is to ensure that you can import a scanned image and get it into a stage that can be used in Photoshop. Scan your calligraphy at 300dpi and save the two or three lines and the large letter as two separate TIFF files.

Step-by-step example

1 *Open a new document using* File>**New**. *Let's stick with a format of 10 inches by 10 inches, a resolution of 300 pixels/inch and RGB colour mode.*

2 *Open the image file that has your scanned two or three lines of calligraphy. Use the* Rectangular Marquee *tool to select the text. Apply the command* Edit>**Copy**.

3 *Activate the window of the new document and apply* Edit>**Paste**. *Your calligraphy is now imported into your work area as a new layer. Move the calligraphy around with the Move tool to cenre it on the canvas.*

4 *If the lettering is too large to fit the canvas you will have to reduce it in size. From the main menu select* Edit>Transform>**Scale**. *This will create a marquee around the pasted text with little square 'handles'. Dragging any of these handles will change the size and proportion of your lettering. To constrain the aspect ratio (the correct proportion), hold down Shift as you drag one of the corners toward the centre. Don't forget to double-click to accept the resizing of the selection. We will deal with transformations in more depth later.*

5 *You will not yet be able to adjust the colour of the calligraphy or apply a style to it. From the main menu apply the command* Select>**Color Range**. *In the Color Range window use the* Eyedropper *tool to select the black of your lettering. Click OK. This will put a selection marquee around the edges of all the letters.*

5a

5b

5c

6 Select Layer>New Fill Layer>**Solid Color**. This will bring up the Color Picker and add a fill layer to the Layers *palette*. Your calligraphy will change to the default colour in the Color Picker. Temporarily close the Color Picker. Double-clicking on the layer's thumbnail in the Layers *palette* will display the Color Picker *again* and let you change the colour of the lettering.

7 Note that you haven't actually filled the lettering with colour. You have created a layer that sits on top. Use the Move tool to drag the coloured calligraphy to below the black.

8 Repeat the process in steps 5 to 7 but this time drag the coloured lettering so that it is above the black.

9 Create a colour layer for the black lettering and set it to black. Delete the original.

10 Open the file with the single calligraphic letter. Cut and paste it into the image. In the Layers palette move the layer to the bottom so that the other lettering lies over the large letter.

11 Now scale and colour the large letter to complete the exercise.

6a

6b

7

8

10

11

Ce que n'est pas bon pour soi,
N'est pas bon pour les autres,
n'est pas bon pour soi,
pas bon pour les autres,
n'est pas bon pour soi,
N'est pas bon pour les autres,

Although in theory any of the brush or pen tools available in Photoshop can be used for creating digital calligraphy, in practice the most satisfactory effects will be achieved by using tools that can emulate the traditional calligraphic broad-edged pen. If you start with this, and fully understand its dynamics, then you can have almost infinite control over the type of line that the tool will make. I have already hinted that Photoshop is not the ideal software for creating original formal calligraphy and that it is more suited to freer, creative work that depends much, for effect, on the overall visual impact. But that is not to say that Photoshop's calligraphic tools are useless. You will find that learning to set and use the Brush tool with the perspective of a calligrapher can add a new dimension to the functionality of the program.

The key to success is knowing where the range of *Brush* tool options can be found, adjusted, and applied. Clicking on the *Brushes* tab on the *Palette Well* while the *Brush* tool is selected will display the options window. One of the tool setting options will be highlighted, depending upon that used last. Select the *Brush Tip Shape*

Creating calligraphy with Photoshop's calligraphic tools

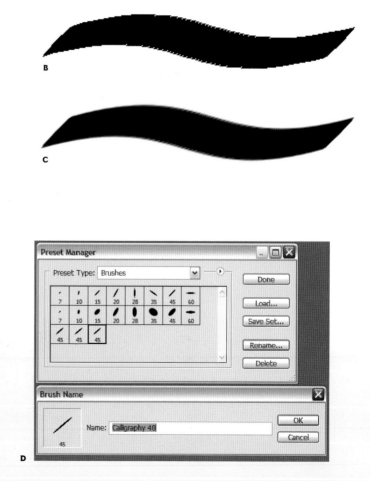

option and make sure that none of the others is selected. This will display an array of brush tip types. You could start with any of these but it will be simpler if you start with one that resembles the tip of a calligraphic broad-edged pen. *Hard Elliptical 45* is a good choice. This will create thicks and thins like those that you will find in a good italic script.

There are several brush tip options that equate with those of a traditional pen nib and the way you use it. *Diameter* is the same as pen nib width and is set by the slider. *Angle* is the pen tip writing angle (the pen angle):

you can either type this in directly or rotate the arrow in the pen angle thumbnail. *Roundness* is the thickness of the nib, which should always be set to zero. Setting *Hardness* at 100% will create a hard-edged calligraphic line. By reducing the percentage the line becomes 'fuzzy-edged'. With some restraint, this effect can simulate ink on paper. If *Spacing* is set to anything other than 1%, the line will be broken, rather than continuous. The brush shape preview tells you the effect of setting these parameters. Any brush that you create can be named and saved as a preset for later use.

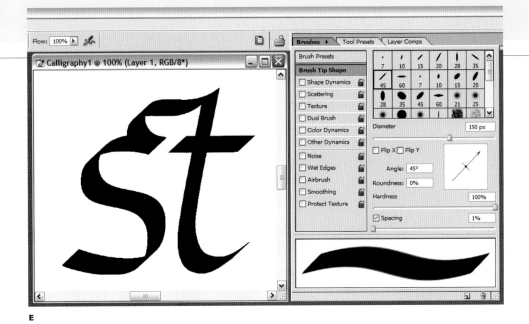

E

F

A *Many of the brush presets are calligraphic in form. Note that even if you name a new brush and it appears on the list, the thumbnail will have the label of the original brush that you modified. However, the pop-up will display the new name.*

B *Even if the colour mode is set to 1 bit black and white (line), and if the hardness of the brush is set to 100%, the edge of the stroke is still not entirely smooth.*

C *Photoshop's so-called hard edge is actually rather soft. In RGB there is a slight softening that is most noticeable on enlargement.*

D *The Preset Manager (Edit>**Preset Manager**) allows you to name and rename modified or custom brushes.*

E *Set the pen nib width (the brush Diameter) and angle to suit the calligraphic style that you plan to use.*

F *When you have adjusted the angle and size of the brush it can be named and saved by clicking on the icon at the bottom of the Brushes palette and entering the new name in the dialog box.*

In Part One I emphasized the importance of the scale and proportions of letters and the way they are written by calligraphers using traditional methods and materials. When you create calligraphy on the computer with Photoshop (or any other graphics software) most of the principles remain the same and some of the techniques can usefully be applied to digital methods. Both of these will be illustrated in the following two exercises. In the first, you can explore freely the effects created by a digital calligraphic brush. By so doing you will discover the potential and pitfalls of the Photoshop tool.

CALLIGRAPHY ON SCREEN

Step-by-step example: informal script

52

1 *Start a new document. Set the resolution to 200 pixels/inch. Create a calligraphic brush in the* Brushes *palette. In the* Brush Tip Shape *dialog box, set the* Diameter *to 60px (pixels), the* Angle *to 35°, the* Roundness *to 0%, the* Hardness *to 100%, and the* Spacing *to 1%.*

2 *With the brush you have created, and using either your mouse or digital pen, write a few zigzags. Try to keep the lines as straight as possible and the distance between the peaks and troughs about the same. Write some wave patterns. You will find that with a mouse it is best to write quickly and spontaneously, rather than taking time to slowly 'construct' the shapes. A digital pen is more controllable if it is used with a fair amount of pressure on the tablet.*

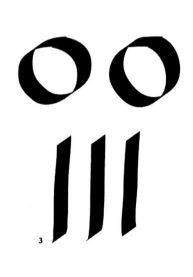

1

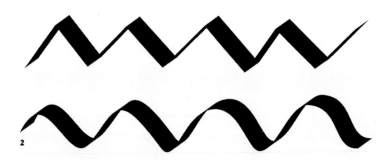

2

3

4

3 *Now write some circles and vertical lines. You may find it difficult at first to judge where the circle closes and to keep the vertical lines straight.*

4 *We will now try writing a few words. Write some words using all lowercase letters as shown in the example to create a very heavy or bold effect. Don't worry if you are not a calligrapher and are not entirely sure about the calligraphic forms of the letters. Use your own handwriting instead. Try to write the letters quickly and rhythmically and in one continuous line if possible. You may have to write it several times before you get an effect with which you are happy. Right away you will see the problem of making the letters too small in relation to the width of the brush tip. The counters of letters such as 'p' and 'o' are closed up and others are illegible.*

5 *Change the Diameter of the brush tip to 25px and write the word again. This time the problem is pen control. It is not easy to maintain an even flow of the brush and keep the forms of the letters consistent. In future sections I will suggest ways of overcoming these problems.*

6 *Change the brush tip Diameter back to 60px. Write the word again, this time with 'normal' proportions similar to the illustration. You will now see the relationship between brush tip diameter and letter height and its vital importance in the creation of good letterform.*

7 *Using Edit>Transform> **Scale**, reduce the width of your word to make a much more condensed form. Add a touch of colour and use an offset colour layer to add interest to the design.*

5

6

7

If you are fairly new to Photoshop, then guides and grids are something that you could easily overlook. We saw in Part One how calligraphers draw a range of guides when they are planning calligraphy. We also saw how to calculate the optimum letter height for any pen nib width. In this example we will apply similar techniques and use Photoshop's guides to help keep lettering regular in height and in a straight line, problems that you may have encountered in the previous exercise. If you are not a calligrapher, this will help you create formal calligraphic lettering using script typefaces as a guide.

CALLIGRAPHY ON SCREEN

Step-by-step example: formal calligraphy

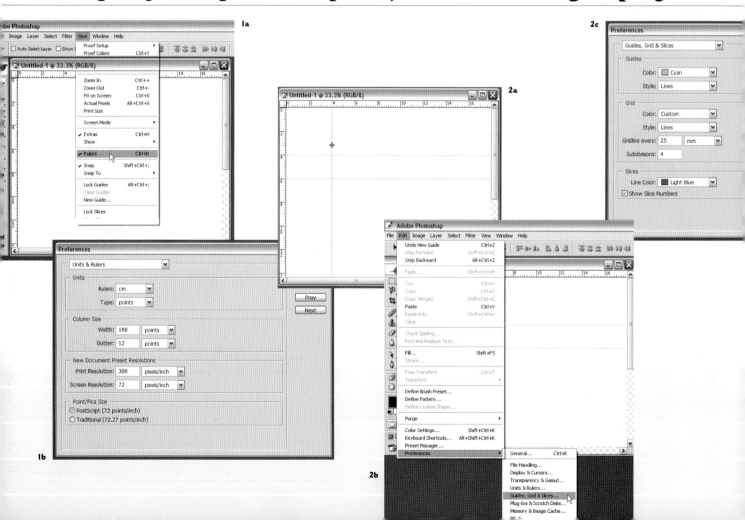

1 Set up a new document. In order to display guides on your image you must have the rulers set to 'on' (View> **Rulers** and make sure that the option is checked). You can set the preferences using Edit>Preferences>**Units & Rulers**, so that you can use metric, imperial, points, or some other unit of measurement.

2 Guides are created by dragging them from the horizontal or vertical rulers and out onto the image, then removed by dragging them off. Use Edit>Preferences> **Guides, Grid & Slices**, or double-click on an existing guide to display the Preferences

dialog box. The colour of the guides is entirely up to you but don't choose black or a colour that is too dark or you may find it distracting.

3 Drag four horizontal rulers onto your canvas, one for the top of the ascender, one for the top of the x-height, one for the bottom of the x-height, and one for the bottom of the descender of the calligraphy that you are going to write.

4 With the Brush tool selected in the Toolbox, create a calligraphic brush in the Brushes palette. This time the choice of most settings is entirely up to you. However, you must set the angle to 90°.

5 Using the Brush tool and marking off little rectangles, measure the ascender, x-height, and descender guides. As we will be writing an italic form, the ideal x-height is about 4½ times the brush tip width. In our example either the pen width is too great or the guides are much too close together and these need to be altered.

6 We will change the brush tip width but you could equally well drag the guides further apart.

7 Unfortunately, Photoshop doesn't let you change the vertical or horizontal angles of its guides. You could create temporary guides using the Pen tool but remember that these have to be deleted before you can perform any transformations on your design. Simply draw sloping guides with the Pen tool, adjust the angle using the Direct Selection tool and copy as many as you think will be useful. If you draw these on a separate layer, they can easily be deleted later.

8 It is now time to write some formal calligraphy – but only a few letters at this stage. Reset your brush angle to 40° but leave all the other settings as they are. Try to follow the italic example illustrated. You will see that the ascender guide has been raised to suit the lettering style.

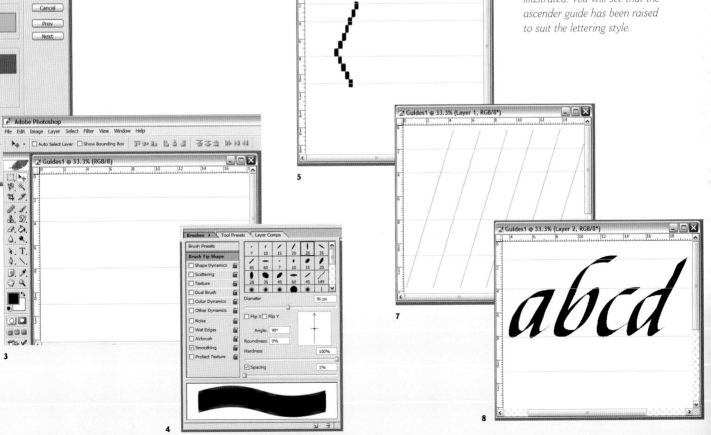

If you are unfamiliar with basic calligraphic styles then there are many books that you can consult that will provide you with excellent examples. There is nothing like learning from example and there is no shortage of good examples in print. Don't expect to become an expert calligrapher overnight. The skill of the expert is learned over many, many years. The great thing about using the computer for calligraphy is that it can maximize the visual impact of even the most mundane lettering through the application of effects making use of Photoshop's filters and other features.

Even so, there is a way that the uninitiated can create satisfactory calligraphic lettering. This is by tracing script or calligraphic typefaces. This is not plagiarism but simply a way to use the typeface as a model for your own calligraphy. No matter how hard you try, your lettering will be different from the typeface original.

Begin by typing your text in a suitable size on a separate layer. Use a light colour so that the type will be clearly distinguished from your writing. Set the brush tip diameter and angle to dimensions that will create a line of the same thickness as the typeface. When you trace,

CALLIGRAPHY ON SCREEN

Other brush-related considerations

56

Lucida

A

A *A good way to create calligraphy on the computer if you are not a calligrapher is to trace over script or calligraphic typefaces. Choose a suitable script typeface. This is Lucida Calligraphy that has been condensed (made narrower) using a transformation in Photoshop.*

B *Carefully trace over the letters with the brush set to match the linear form of the typeface.*

C *Adjust the letter spacing and remove the original typeface.*

Lucida

B

Lucida

C

carefully follow the centre line of the letters with your brush. After you have completed the tracing, remove or hide the original typed lettering layer. You will find that some adjustment to spacing and letterforms will be needed. Tracing typefaces is a very simple and useful technique for those of you who need some guidance on calligraphic letterforms.

You can experiment with the other effects available through the options on the left side of the *Brushes* window but they are of doubtful value for calligraphy. The exception to this is the *Control* setting under *Shape Dynamics*. For those of you with a graphics tablet and digital pen, setting this control to *Pen Pressure* will vary the calligraphic line, making it broader when you press hard and narrower when you press less hard on the stylus.

With practice, a skill in utilizing this technique can be developed. However, in so doing, the thick and thin effect of the broad-edged pen is lost.

It is a relatively simple procedure to create your own brush in Photoshop. Whether this will be better for calligraphic use than modifying the presets through the *Brushes* palette is doubtful. However, if you would like to try creating your own calligraphic brush then firstly draw a simple thin line with the *Brush* tool that resembles one of the preset brush tips (or any other shape you choose). Select the shape you have drawn with the *Rectangular Marquee* tool. Apply the command *Edit>***Define Brush Preset** from the main menu. This will now let you name your new brush. It can then be used and modified like any of the other brushes.

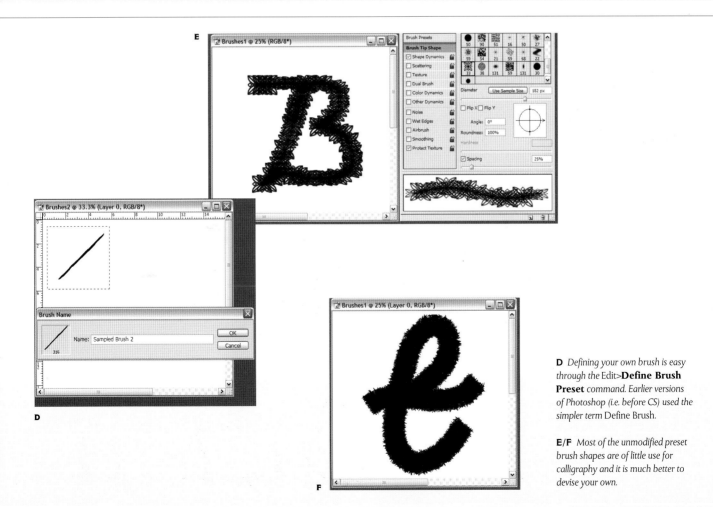

D *Defining your own brush is easy through the* Edit>**Define Brush Preset** *command. Earlier versions of Photoshop (i.e. before CS) used the simpler term* Define Brush.

E/F *Most of the unmodified preset brush shapes are of little use for calligraphy and it is much better to devise your own.*

TRANSFORMATIONS & PA

Scale, proportion, and orientation

58

A When you enlarge a section of an image using a scale transformation, the pixelation can become conspicuous. In these cases it would be better to rewrite the scaled-up word to retain sharpness.

B Flipped lettering can be used for some effects including reflection. Here a copy of the word has been flipped vertically, skewed, and coloured differently from the original word.

C The original, a 180° rotation, a 90° clockwise rotation, and a 90° counterclockwise rotation.

D An image or selection can be rotated by a specific amount using the Arbitrary rotation procedure.

E Flipping calligraphy vertically or horizontally mirrors the lettering.

F To enlarge or reduce the image or selection and retain correct proportions, drag one of the corner handles toward or away from the centre while holding down the Shift key.

G To reduce (condense) or increase (expand) the image or selection width, drag any of the handles toward or away from the centre without holding Shift.

H When calligraphy is transformed by scaling and reducing the width to a considerable degree, the vertical stress decreases creating an uneven weight throughout the lettering.

Frequently you will come across situations when you want to change the scale or proportions of all or some of your lettering design. To do this, Photoshop uses transformations. This should not be confused with resampling your image so that you can change its resolution and, to some extent, control its quality. When you transform a design or part of it in any way the number of pixels remains the same, either within the whole image or within the selection. Therefore, if you double the size of an area within a 300 pixels/inch image using a scale transformation from 100 by 100 pixels to

200 by 200 pixels the effect on the selected part is to make it appear as if it is at a resolution of only 150 pixels/inch. If this sounds mathematically complicated, look at the illustration (F) in which the first word of the text has been enlarged by transforming a selection. Note how much more conspicuous the pixels are. When you perform transformations, you must be aware of this effect and ensure that you are working at a sufficiently high resolution to accommodate the potential loss of quality.

The simplest transformations that you may want to use in digital calligraphy include rotating, flipping, making all or part of it larger or smaller, and increasing or decreasing the height to width ratio. In typography this latter distortion is referred to as condensing or expanding.

To rotate the whole image you simply select *Image*>**Rotate Canvas** from the main drop-down menu. This presents several alternatives including the fixed rotations of *180°, 90° clockwise, 90° counterclockwise* and *Arbitrary*. In the case of the *Arbitrary* option, a specific rotation in degrees is entered in a pop-up dialog box. You should always give careful thought to the effect on legibility of changing the orientation of your lettering from the horizontal. The further you move from the normal reading line the less legible it will be. Using the *Flip Canvas Horizontal* or *Flip Canvas Vertical* commands has quite a different effect on the lettering. Applying these procedures mirrors the image. You may think there is little use for this option but it has possibilities – to create the effect of a reflection or shadow, for example.

In contrast with the above procedures, the *Edit*> **Transform** command can be applied to the whole image, a layer, a selection, and in the form *Edit*>**Transform Path**, to a path. Applying the procedure to an image or layer without first making a selection creates a transformation marquee around it. Using any of the selection tools to create a selection creates a transformation marquee around the selection. The marquee has eight handles that can be dragged to new positions to scale, condense, or expand your lettering or part of it. When you condense lettering you will notice that the vertical lines become thinner, increasing the horizontal weight. This affects the evenness of the calligraphy. Avoid excessive condensing of the letterforms.

F

G

H

Perspective can be simulated using the *Edit>Transform> Perspective* procedure on a selection. The degree to which this is effective depends on the nature of your design. Sometimes you will get a real perspective effect, sometimes the effect will be less satisfactory. The perspective viewpoint can be above, below, or at either side of the selected shape. If you think of each of the handles as the perspective vanishing point you will get a rough idea of what is happening when you drag the handles in various directions. You can even use the corner handles to apply perspective in various directions at once.

From a calligraphic point of view, one of the most useful transformations is *Edit>Transform>Skew*. This command lets you increase or decrease the slope of your lettering. After creating the transformation marquee, drag the centre top handle to the right. This will increase the lettering slope. Similarly, dragging the handle to the left will decrease the slope, even to the extent that it slopes backward. Be careful with back-sloping calligraphy. This can create very negative visual impact. Dragging the side centre handles will skew the lettering vertically. Of course if you skew several lines of text simultaneously, the left

Other simple transformations

60

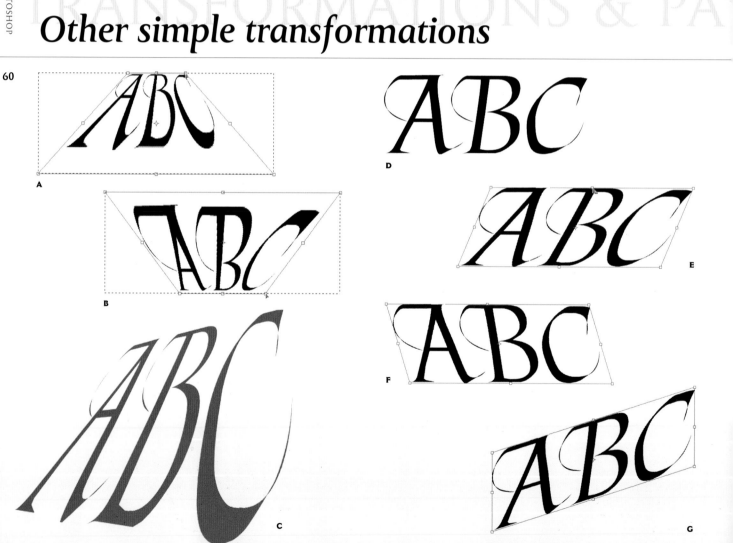

A

B

C

D

E

F

G

and right margins will also be skewed. You will then have to adjust each line if you want to have an even vertical left or right margin.

If you make a path using any of Photoshop's vector tools, then go to *Edit* on the main menu, and you will see that it offers *Transform Path* instead of simply *Transform*. This will appear even if you have made a selection on your image. The transformations that can be applied to images and selections can also be applied to paths.

I have described the different settings of the *Transform* command to demonstrate the effects that each can create. You will probably want to combine these effects in some way at some point. An alternative to the simple *Transform* command is the *Edit>**Free Transform*** procedure. Through it you can make all the transformations that I've described.

These operations can be performed with *Free Transform*:

Scaling – Drag any of the eight handles to increase or decrease the size of the image or selection. Hold down shift to constrain the proportions.

Flipping – Drag one handle past the opposite handle.

Rotating – Rotate the image or selection by dragging outside the marquee. You will see that the cursor changes to a curved double arrow.

Skewing – Holding down control and dragging a side handle will skew the image or selection.

Distorting – Holding down control and dragging a corner handle will let you distort the image or selection.

Don't forget that you must double-click within the marquee to accept any of the transformations that you have made with either procedure.

A/B *Very simple perspective effects can be achieved through the transformation procedures. Different viewpoints can be used.*

C *Using different viewpoints simultaneously can make a more complex perspective effect.*

D/E *Lettering can be italicized by using skew transformations.*

F *Back-sloping lettering should be used with caution.*

G *Lettering can be skewed vertically as well as horizontally.*

H/I *When several lines are skewed at the same time, the margins are also skewed and these have to be readjusted line by line.*

The extent of the degradation of image quality when using transformations depends on the resolution of the image and the degree to which the transformations are applied. The loss of quality that you will get with slight adjustments of lettering at 600 pixels/inch will be barely noticeable. As calligraphy usually relies for its effectiveness on the sharpness of the writing, transformations must be used with great care. There could be occasions when you want to make use of the exaggerated pixelation effect that you get when you use transformations at lower resolutions. The contrast between a 'fuzzy' image and one that is very crisp and sharp can be very effective. It is with these reservations that we now consider more bizarre transformation effects.

It is so easy to create interesting and unusual effects with computer graphics software that we can often lose sight of the aims of our artistic endeavors. From time to time take a step back and ask yourself how you would like your calligraphy to be interpreted by others. When we come to apply distortion to calligraphy 'losing sight of the aims' is often literally what we are doing. By distorting something that could be perfectly well-formed lettering,

TRANSFORMATIONS & PA

Distortion

A *The undistorted letter.*

B/C *Drag any of the corner handles of a transformation marquee to distort the selection.*

D *When you use a perspective transformation some interesting effects can be achieved by pulling a handle beyond the opposite side of the marquee.*

we are creating something else that may or may not have the desired effect. Many distortion techniques can generate visual impact and, if this is your aim, all is well. Be careful, however, with any calligraphy that you want your audience to be able to read with ease, when it is desirable to retain maximum legibility.

Distortions are made by dragging any of the corner handles of a transformation marquee, either in *Edit* > *Transform* > **Distort**, or in *Edit* > **Free Transform** while holding down the Control key. The selection or image is stretched or shrunk in the direction of the drag. You can drag the handle in and out and in any direction by either method. Double-click within the marquee when you are satisfied with the result or use *Undo* if you want to return to the unaltered form.

Some very unusual effects can be created by dragging handles beyond the opposite boundary of the marquee while using the *Distort* or *Perspective* options. In both instances, parts of the image are flipped and distorted. If your original image is calligraphic in form, the distortions will retain the calligraphic effect. Usually, however, the images are almost abstract and are hardly recognizable as the original written forms.

You can have some fun with transformations. Experiment using combinations of two or more different methods. Try using both the individual transformations under *Edit* > **Transform** and the more flexible method using *Edit* > **Free Transform**.

E *Similarly, pulling a handle beyond the opposite side of the marquee while in Distort mode can create new abstract calligraphic forms.*

F *This image was created using a combination of several transformation techniques. The 'fuzzy' background form has been overlaid with a sharp capital 'A' that has been mirrored to produce a balanced design.*

63

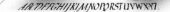

D

E

F

We will delay delving into the complexities of vector graphics and definitions of the differences between them and bitmaps. As an introduction to vector paths, we will work on an exercise in which they are used as another method of creating original calligraphy on the computer. As with all of its vector handling functions, Photoshop's vector methods are rather limited and cumbersome to use for calligraphy. A creative approach to their application is required to enhance their functionality. You may find this method useful.

Understanding stroke

1 Start a new document with a resolution of 300 pixels per inch. You will be writing a word of your choice so, if you wish, drag down guidelines for the ascender, x-height, and descender as described in a previous section. The distance the guides are apart doesn't matter at this stage. Select the Freeform Pen tool from the Toolbox.

2 Write a word very freely using the pen. The line will be only one pixel wide. Use the Direct Selection tool and drag a selection over your word. This will display the anchor points along the path. The number of anchor points will depend, to some extent, upon how quickly you wrote the word. The faster you wrote, the fewer anchor points there will be.

3 However quickly you wrote the word, you will almost certainly have too many anchor points. Use the Delete Anchor Point tool to remove unnecessary points. Use the Convert Anchor Point tool and the Direct Selection tool to adjust the path until you are happy with the lettering. You may have to refer to one of the next sections for help on this procedure if you are not already familiar with Photoshop's vector tools. Create a new layer.

4 Select a calligraphic brush in the Brushes palette. The brush tip width doesn't matter at this point. In the Paths palette click on the Stroke Path with Brush tab at the bottom.

5 Your word will be converted into a calligraphic script based on the brush parameters that you selected.

Photoshop's basic path creation tools work well and writing a calligraphic path with the *Freeform Pen* tool is simplicity itself. With a mouse or digital pen you can write spontaneously and Photoshop instantly makes a path (or paths), complete with anchor points ready for you to modify. This path can then be 'stroked' with any brush you choose. The problem occurs when you want to edit the path. If you make adjustments to the path or anchor points, the stroked path doesn't alter. The only way to accommodate your changes is to drag the path to

another part of the screen and apply the stroke again. On the plus side, this lets you restroke the path with a different line thickness. If you restroke over the first one with a narrower brush tip it will be obscured.

6 *You may not be happy with some of the lettering. Make further adjustments to the path. The stroke will not change.*

7 *Drag the path to a clear part of the screen.*

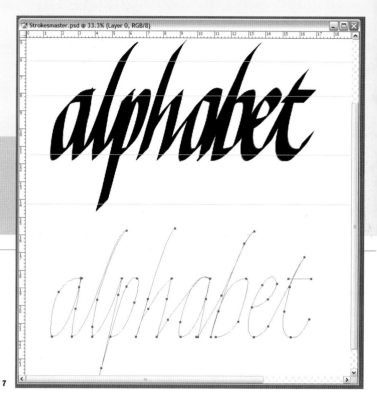

7

5

8 *Apply a stroke again, changing the brush settings if you wish. Delete the layer with the first stroked word. Stroke the path. If you want to make further changes, undo the stroke, alter the path, and stroke the path again. You can repeat this procedure over and over again until you are happy with the result.*

6

8

Photoshop is full of little idiosyncrasies. For example, say you have been using other computer graphics software for a while, and have learned the very simple procedure of filling shapes with the paint bucket. You then spend all your hard-earned cash on Photoshop, start working on a design, select the *Paint Bucket* tool, click on the area that you want to fill, and it doesn't work! You then read that you can fill an area using the Backspace key and you ask yourself where on earth is the logic to that? In many cases, the difficulties that Photoshop creates for the user arise mostly from the

fact that, for most procedures, it offers the user a whole range of ways of performing them – and usually the method you choose lets you down. The reason why a particular procedure doesn't do what you think it should do is usually something very simple. Perhaps you aren't working on the correct layer, a selection isn't active, or you are attempting to do something on a type layer that has to be rasterized first. It is useful to keep a list of things to check when something doesn't work so that you can go through the possibilities to resolve the problem. This is very much the case with fills.

Understanding fill

A

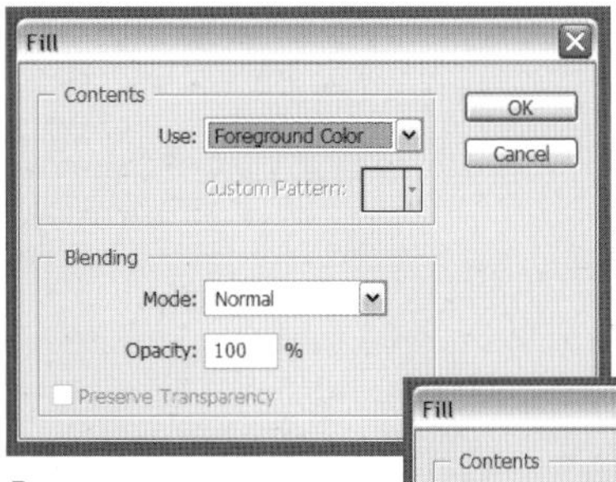

B

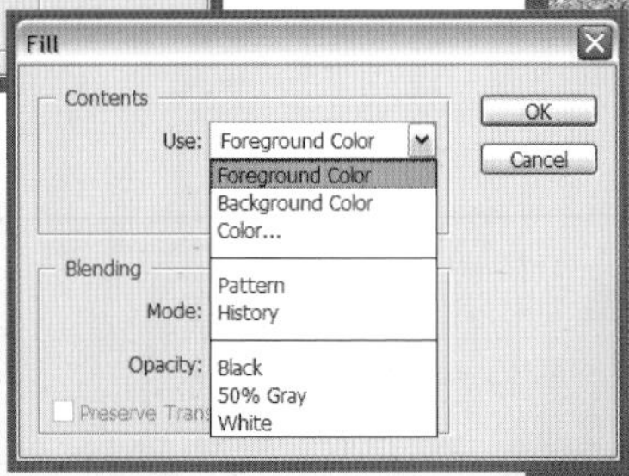

C

D

Filling is putting a colour or pattern inside a shape. The edges of the shape that is being filled have certain properties that permit or prevent the fill colour or pattern spreading beyond the boundary. The degree to which this happens is controlled by *Tolerance*. A *Tolerance* of 0 obstructs any fill colour. A *Tolerance* of 100 lets the colour spread indefinitely. These figures are theoretical and, in practice, 0 allows some colour to spread and a setting of less than 100 will prevent colour from filling. Because it is so imprecise, some professional users of Photoshop dismiss the *Paint Bucket* as a useless tool. For most of our calligraphic applications, however, it is probably the most convenient, although it cannot be used in bitmap mode. The other important fill parameter is *Opacity*. This controls the density of the fill colour. Repeatedly applying a fill with the *Opacity* set low will gradually build up the colour density. Both these features are set in the *Options bar*. For other *Paint Bucket* fill options check your Photoshop manual.

Another way to apply fills is to use *Edit>**Fill***. This will fill a selection. The *Options* window lets you select the fill method. You can set the *Opacity* but, as you are filling a selection, you cannot set the *Tolerance*.

Finally, the illogical Backspace key will fill a selection with the background colour. This removes pixels on a layer and, if the selection is floating, the Backspace key will delete it. For this reason it is better to use Control+Backspace. You can fill with the foreground colour by pressing Alt+Backspace. With this method you can set *Tolerance* and some other parameters.

A *The* Options bar *lets you control the settings of the* Paint Bucket *tool.*

B *Using the command* Edit>**Fill** *displays the* Fill *options window.*

C *The drop-down menu in the* Fill *options window lets you set the type of fill that you want to use.*

D *Colour and pattern fills enhance even the simplest of images.*

E *A simple gradient fill. To illustrate* Tolerance, *we will try and fill the lighter, left-hand colour with black.*

F *Using the* Paint Bucket *tool with* Tolerance *set to 1 produces a fill in a very restricted area of the gradient.*

G *Setting the* Tolerance *to 100 permits the* Paint Bucket *fill to spread over much more of the gradient.*

E

F

G

Photoshop is a bitmap-based program. In simple terms, it works with images described as a set of dots, points, or pixels. It also has some vector manipulation features, one of which we have already seen when we drew a path with the *Freeform Pen* tool and manipulated the path before applying strokes. When you enlarge a bitmap letter the pixelation becomes more evident. However, because vector graphics are described mathematically and the image is drawn on the screen after the calculations are made, enlarging a letter will retain the sharp, smooth edges, irrespective of its size.

One difference between bitmaps and vectors is how you modify and manipulate them. Bitmap shapes can only be changed by moving, adding, or removing pixels. Although Photoshop can perform scale, skew, and other graphic effects easily on bitmaps, the procedure is still based on moving, adding, or removing pixels. With vector shapes, the lines and curves can be manipulated in various ways and with accuracy difficult to achieve with bitmaps.

We have to understand some definitions before progressing. Photoshop's terminology is similar to, but not identical with, that of other programs. A path, with which

Bitmaps and vectors

A *Vector shapes or letters (left) retain their smooth edge irrespective of the degree of enlargement. The pixelation effect on bitmaps (right) increases as the image is enlarged.*

B *A simple straight segment with two anchor points.*

C *A curved segment with three anchor points and symmetrical control handles.*

D *With a cusp point the control handles can be adjusted independently.*

E *The* Pen *tool flyout.*

F *The* Direct Selection *tool flyout.*

G *One way to create a path based on a letter is to use the* Freeform Pen *tool with the* Magnetic *box checked in the* Option *bar.*

H *A path is formed as you trace the outline of the letter. The tool doesn't have to be placed right on the edge: it will jump and attach itself to the outline as long as it isn't too far away.*

A

anchor point

B

cusp point

smooth point

control handle

C

D

you will now be familiar, is made up of a series of straight or curved segments. Straight segments are simply two end points, nodes, or anchor points. A curved segment has one or more anchor points with control handles that can be dragged to alter the shape of the curves. Anchor points can be changed to various forms using Photoshop's *Convert Anchor Point* tool. These include a corner point, which is the corner between two straight segments; a smooth point, which has two symmetrical control handles; and a cusp point, which has two independent control handles. In certain modes the curve of the path itself can be shaped without using the anchor points or control handles.

Paths are drawn using either of the *Pen* tools in the flyout of the *Toolbox*, the *Freeform Pen* tool and the simple *Pen* tool, which you probably won't use much for

calligraphy. The *Pen* tool flyout also includes the *Add Anchor Point*, *Delete Anchor Point*, and *Convert Anchor Point* tools. You will have to select these repeatedly when working with vectors, a very frustrating aspect of Photoshop's vector procedures. The *Direct Selection* tool is used to manipulate paths and anchor points and the *Path Selection* tool does exactly what it says. Paths can be open or closed. If a path is to be converted to a selection outline, it will have to be closed by clicking again on the first point of the path.

Another vector procedure that you may find useful is to select the *Freeform Pen* tool and then check *Magnetic* in the *Options bar*. This will work as if you have combined the *Magnetic Lasso* tool with the *Freeform Pen* tool and by tracing close to the edge of your letter or shape you can create a path complete with anchor points.

It is perhaps misleading to suggest that you can convert a bitmap image to a vector drawing. Bitmaps remain as pixel-by-pixel bitmaps no matter what you do to them. What Photoshop lets you do is to trace around areas in a bitmap image – in our case calligraphic letterforms – then convert that tracing to one or more paths. Although this can be done in various ways, there are really only two that are practical. These are demonstrated in the following step-by-step examples and you can choose which method you prefer to work with in the future, or which is more appropriate on any given occasion.

Converting bitmap to vector

1

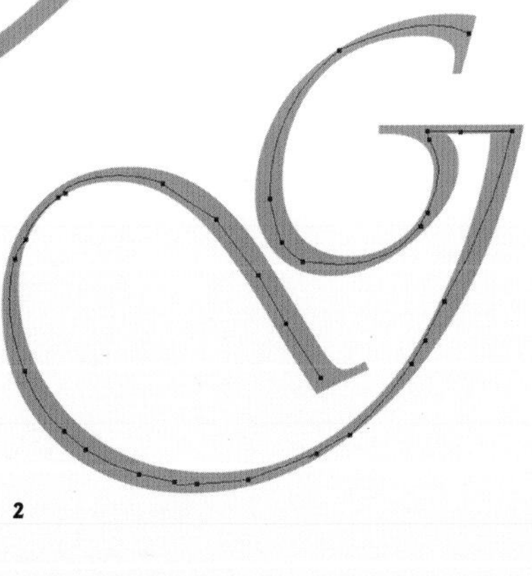

2

3

4

5

6

7a

1 For the first example we will recap on the method of creating calligraphy by tracing a typeface. This time, we will use the Freeform Pen *tool* to copy the linear form of a letter and stroke the path that we make. This will be used as the basis for the bitmap to vector conversion. Type a calligraphic letter in a large size. In this case, 600 point Vivaldi capitals.

2 Using the Freeform Pen *tool*, draw a vector path by following the center line of the letter. Don't be concerned if this is not accurate.

3 You will have far too many anchor points. Use the Delete Anchor Point *tool* to remove all the unnecessary ones. The fewer points that you can leave that will still describe the form of the letter, the better. Use this tool and the Direct Selection *tool* to adjust the path to a smooth flowing line. Use the Convert Anchor Point *tool* regularly to adjust smooth curves.

4 Drag the path away from the original typed letter. Delete the letter.

5 Set the Brush Tip in the Brushes *palette* to a width and angle of your choice and stroke the letter as described earlier. This will produce your very own calligraphic form of the typeface. It is important to realize at this point that the stroked letter is a bitmap and not a vector image. The vector path is quite separate.

6 Delete the path. We will now convert the letter to vectors. Select the letter with the Magic Wand *tool*.

7 In the Paths *palette* click on Make Work Path from Selection *(at the bottom of the palette)*. This will create a vector path around the outline of the letter.

8 Delete the calligraphic letter to reveal the path that can now be modified, manipulated, and filled with a colour or pattern.

9 We will now work through an example using the technique mentioned in the previous section in which the Freeform Pen *tool* is used with the Magnetic *setting* enabled. Start with a new typed letter.

10 Select the Freeform Pen *tool* and check the Magnetic *setting box* on the Options bar.

11 Trace around the edge of the letter, keeping the tool close to the edges. Don't forget to trace any counters of the letter as well.

12 A vector path is now formed around the outline of the letter.

13 Delete the letter to leave the work path.

7b

8

9

10

11

12

13

ow that you are able to create vectors from a bitmap shape, the forms of these calligraphic letters can be corrected and improved. Although it is not ideally suited to the purpose, Photoshop still lets you use this approach, making it much easier to reshape letters or parts of letters than by the bitmap method of pixel-by-pixel drawing. In this exercise we will use vectors to create simple flourishes on a letter.

Calligraphic flourishing is the technique in which certain parts of letters are extended to create some sort of effect. This can be both functional and decorative.

Modifying lettering using vectors

72

1 *With the* Brush *tool set to a 'broad-edged pen' shape, write the capital 'R' using a mouse or stylus – several times, if you wish, until you are happy with the form. Don't worry about slight 'wiggles'. Alternatively, import a scanned letter.*

2 *In Photoshop there are several ways of creating paths from bitmap shapes, including the* Magnetic Lasso *tool, the* Freeform Pen *tool, and the* Pen *tool. In this example, we will use the simplest method and make a work path from a selection.*

3 *Select the letter by using the* Magic Wand *tool (click on the letter). This will create a selection mask that follows the outline of the letter. In the* Paths *palette, click* Make Work Path *from* Selection. *This changes the selection mask to a vector path comprising segments and anchor points. Adjust the vectors as necessary. You will almost certainly have far too many anchor points and these must be reduced using the* Delete Anchor Point *tool. Ensure that you retain anchor points at corners and other places in the outline where the direction of the vector line changes significantly. Remember that if you remove an anchor point by mistake you can always undo.*

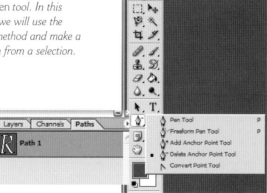

It can be used on the initial letter at the beginning of a section of text for emphasis, or we may want to fill out a line of text by extending part of the last letter. Flourishing was employed extensively for decoration by calligraphers in copybooks in the seventeenth and eighteenth centuries, although it was often overused. When you create flourishes you should try to keep the form of the lettering and retain its legibility.

When working with vectors, there are several points you should keep in mind. The fewer anchor points that you have, the smoother the outline of your letter shape will be. On the other hand, if you have too few anchor points, the lettering could be very geometric and lifeless. Use the fewest number of anchor points that will let you create the desired subtlety in the letterform. Flourishes can usually be defined with very few anchor points, while the use of terminal serifs can increase the number of necessary anchor points significantly. Digital type designers ensure that direction lines are always vertical or horizontal. Although much of the time this can help to control the shape of calligraphic letters, a more cursive form will result if this unwritten rule is not strictly followed.

LETTERFORM

4 *Note that the counter of the letter is a separate path from the outer path. Here we will separate the 'leg' of the capital 'R'. Delete two anchor points at the top of the 'leg' to separate the paths and close both paths by dragging one anchor point over the other.*

5 *We will now 'flourish' the top part of the 'leg' of the letter. Drag and adjust the anchor points as shown. To make the line look more calligraphic, ensure that it tapers to a very thin line.*

6 *Similarly, flourish the top line of the letter as shown, tapering the curve. Crossing paths at the end of a flourish line can achieve an even more calligraphic effect. We will see how this is done later. Remove*

the serif at the bottom of the letter to complete the process. The paths of the letter can be filled with colour, or a swatch effect applied.

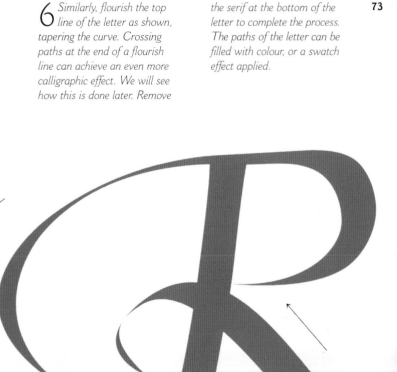

4

5

6

The broad-edged nib on paper produces a line that varies in thickness depending upon the direction in which it's used, if the pen is held at a constant angle. The digital equivalent behaves in exactly the same way. Look closely at expert calligraphy written using a traditional pen and you will see that thick and thin lines do not always appear as you would expect from a broad-edged nib writing at a consistent angle. This is often the case at the end of a descender or flourish. The way this is achieved is by changing the pen angle so that the written line is much more lively. Some calligraphers use the term 'turning the pen'. We cannot do this in Photoshop. We have to resort to adjustments of the vectors to achieve the same effect. This will enhance the calligraphic effect of your lettering. We will explore this through the following step-by-step example.

Using vector adjustments to create or retain a truly calligraphic effect

1 *Open a new document. Write a lowercase letter 'g' and 'e' as in the illustration, using either a calligraphic brush or the* Freeform Pen *tool and stroking the vector path. If you use the latter method, remove the path before proceeding to the next step. You will see that the end of the descender of the 'g' thickens at its extremity because of the pen angle. Similarly, the upturn at the end of the 'e' and its flourish broaden out in a rather unsatisfactory way.*

2 *Select the letters using the* Magic Wand *tool.*

3 *Convert the selection to a path through the* Paths *palette. Click on* Make Work Path from Selection *in the same way as you did in the previous exercise 'Modifying lettering using vectors'. Note that both letters are made up of two paths, one for the outline and the other for the counter.*

4 Delete the original letters to leave just the paths.

5 As before, you will have too many anchor points. Starting with the 'g', reduce the number using the Delete Anchor Point *tool from the* Toolbox. *Ensure that you have only three anchor points at the bottom of the descender, as shown in the illustration.*

6 Make adjustments to the form as necessary using the Direct Selection *tool and, when necessary, the* Convert Anchor Point *tool. Delete one of the two terminal anchor points on the descender.*

7 Using the control handles, adjust the path so that the descender tapers to a spike. The terminal anchor point will have to be a cusp. Try overlapping the paths slightly.

8 Repeat the procedure with the 'e', including the flourished central line.

9 Select the paths with the Path Selection *tool and fill them with black or a solid colour to see the true effect. With some practice you can create a really lively descender and attractive flourish.*

It might appear to be a bit odd to start with black in a section on the use of colour. Strictly speaking, black is not part of the colour spectrum but is a colour in the sense that it is part of the palette of artists and designers, along with white. You will remember that, in our RGB additive colour system, black is the total absence of red, green, and blue, while white is the combination of the three primaries. In historical times, calligraphic text was written in black ink. The browns that we see in some old manuscripts are due to fading or impure colour mixes. Initial letters and other highlighted text were picked out in colour, usually red, or gold. Optimum legibility is achieved when the contrast between the letters is greatest—this means black on white. But we live in a colourful world and the effectiveness of a calligraphic design can be increased through attributes that have little to do with legibility. Photoshop lets you work with millions of colours – so let's use some of them.

While black on white produces the highest level of potential legibility, contrasting pigment primary colours produce the greatest degree of colour contrast. The pigment colour primaries, in the subtractive colour

Working with colour

A *Black on white is the most legible combination of colours.*

B *Black set against a red background is rather lifeless.*

C *White against a flat colour can be very effective.*

D *Primary colours against their opposite colours contrast dramatically, but the effect can be overvibrant and very harsh.*

E *In this series of illustrations the Paint Bucket tool has been used repeatedly with the opacity set to 20%. Each application increases the colour density. This gives great control over basic colour fills.*

A

B

C

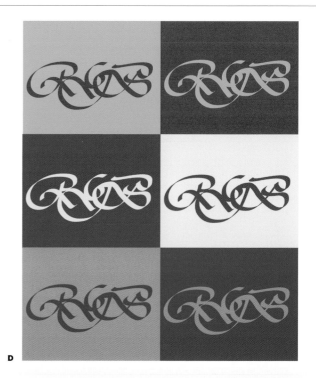

D

E

system, are red, yellow, and blue. Add red to yellow and you get orange, adding blue to red gives purple, and blue and yellow make green. So if we place primary yellow against its opposite, that is purple (red plus blue), the result is a vibrant clash. Similarly, if we place primary blue against orange (yellow plus red) we get a similar effect. The same goes for red against green. This is not to say you should never use these colours together—it all depends upon the effect you want to achieve. Nature finds it easy to use colour schemes like this to great effect, but we are not so smart.

You will probably not want to damage your eyesight or that of anyone else who sees your work and more subtle combinations of colours will be better. If you use nothing but bright, contrasting colours you will communicate less well than when you create emphasis by using bright colours sparingly and selectively.

Opacity can be controlled with most Photoshop tools or commands that add colour to an image. This can be used effectively when you are not certain how strong you want your colour to be – for example, when adding a flat colour behind your calligraphy. Try building up the colour gradually. Once you have chosen a colour, set the opacity to a low level: somewhere between 15% and 25% would be about right. Repeatedly adding colour increases the colour density a little at a time. You can stop when you think the colour is just right.

LIGRAPHY

F *Subtle colours are quiet and easy on the eye. If used badly they can be rather dull.*

F

G *We can learn a lot from manuscripts in which a bright colour is used for emphasis. Here the red lettering is most effective because the other colours have been muted.*

abcdefghijklmnopqrstuvwxyz

G

H *Nature often succeeds where we do not. Although purple and green are opposite colours in the RGB mode, in this passionflower the effect is beautiful.*

H

Calligraphy doesn't require the whole range of colour handling techniques that Photoshop has to offer. It is likely that you will use only a limited selection of the software's mountain of colour adjustment and manipulation procedures in your lettering work. This is not to suggest that you are in any way less sensitive to colour than artists and photographers working with real-world images. It is simply that you do not have to concern yourself with some of the more complex colour controls.

You may be familiar with some of the procedures in the following steps, in which case you can skip this section or use it as a memorandum.

Each of the options can be accessed from the main menu by selecting *Image>***Adjustments** and then the relevant option. Most of these colour adjustments could be used on your final work, although there is no reason why they can't be useful at other stages in the development of your calligraphy.

Basic colour adjustments

78

1 *If you already have a colourful piece of calligraphy use it in the following steps, otherwise prepare a simple piece that uses a range of colours.*

2 *Display the drop-down menu by selecting* Image>**Adjustments**. *You will be presented with some 21 different options. To begin with, we will use only seven.*

3 *Select* Image> Adjustments> **Brightness/Contrast**. *Make sure that you have checked the Preview box. Move the Brightness slider to the right and your image will lighten. Move it to the left and it will darken. Reset the Brightness slider to the middle (zero).*

4 *Move the* Contrast *slider to the right and the contrast of your image will increase. Move it to the left and it will decrease.*

5 *Try adjusting both at the same time and in different directions to see the effect. Cancel the* Brightness/ Contrast *option window.*

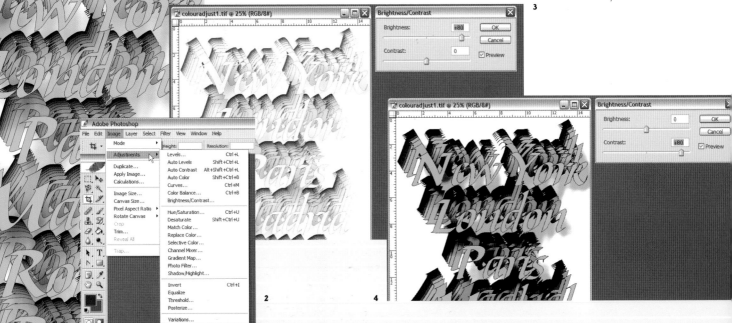

6 *So far, these procedures are simple and the results obvious. Select the* Hue/Saturation *option to display the option window. We will ignore the* Lightness *control, since this does the same as the* Brightness *control that we used before. Move the* Hue *slider to the right and left. You will see that your image changes through the colour spectrum. Hue is the actual colour or 'full intensity tint', to use the official term. Reset the slider to zero.*

7 *Move the* Saturation *slider as far as it will go to the left. Your image appears to have changed to greyscale. In fact it is still an RGB image but the red, green, and blue have been completely removed or de-saturated. Saturation is the actual 'amount' of colour. Cancel the options window.*

8 *Select the* Color Balance *option. Three sliders let you bias the colour of your image in opposite spectral directions. Further options let you control whether your actions take effect on the shadows, midtones, or highlights. When you have experimented with this option, close the window.*

9 *You may remember that Photoshop's RGB colour mode lets you adjust each of the colour channels independently. Although this can be done through separate channel layers, it can also be applied through the* Image>Adjustments> **Channel Mixer** *command. Open the* Channel Mixer *window. Here you can set the* Output Channel *via the drop-down submenu, then adjust its red, green, and blue content.*

In the previous examples, relatively straightforward adjustments were made to the colours of an image. The following group of procedures let you make more dramatic changes to colours, including reductions in the tonal range. Take care in using some of these effects. Although you will have very practical uses for them, giving you yet more control over your calligraphy, avoid the danger of applying unusual effects in inappropriate places.

Other useful colour controls

80

1 *Select a calligraphic image that includes a good selection of colour and tones.*

2 *Once again, we will use the* Image>**Adjustments** *drop-down menu. From this, select Replace Color. This command does exactly what it says – it will replace one colour with another of your choice. The options window has three main parts that you should explore in the first instance. At the top, there are three colour pickers. The one to the far left lets you choose a colour from your image by clicking on it. This will be the colour to replace. The centre one makes a selected colour your foreground colour and the one to the right reverts the foreground colour to the*

previous state. The Fuzziness *slidebar adjusts the extent to which there is a sudden or gradual change from one colour to the other adjacent colours in the image. The* Hue, Saturation, *and* Lightness *slidebars at the bottom of the options window let you create a colour based on the one you have chosen to replace. Select a colour in your calligraphy and use the lower slidebars to make a new colour. Leave the* Fuzziness *set to zero.*

3 *With all the settings left as before, set the* Fuzziness *to 200 (maximum). You will find that there is now a gradual change from one colour to the other. Cancel the options window.*

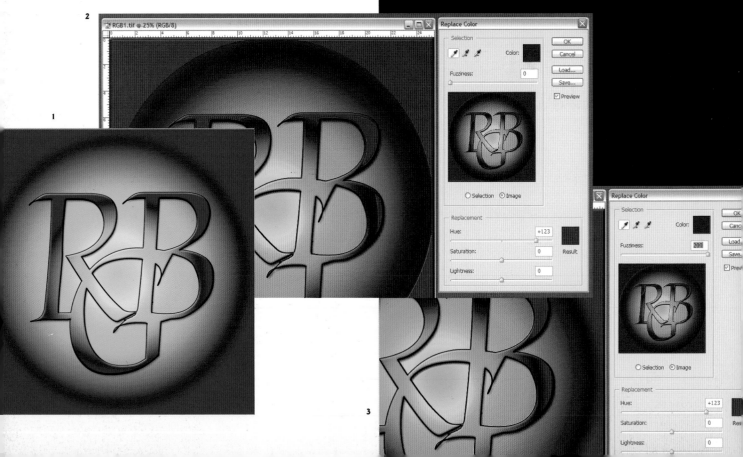

4 *Select the* Photo Filter *option. This procedure works just like a colour filter fitted over a camera lens and produces a colour cast on your image. You can choose one of the preset colours from the drop-down menu (the Filter setting) or click on* colour *to choose any colour from the* Color *palette.*

5 *Selecting* Image> Adjustments>**Invert** *replaces all colours with the RGB opposites. If the image is monochrome, black is replaced by white and white replaced by black. Usually the effect is rather strange but it does have its uses in calligraphy.*

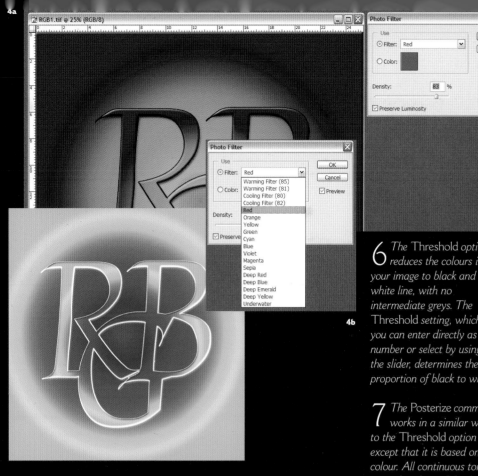

4a

4b

5

6 *The* Threshold *option reduces the colours in your image to black and white line, with no intermediate greys. The* Threshold *setting, which you can enter directly as a number or select by using the slider, determines the proportion of black to white.*

7 *The* Posterize *command works in a similar way to the* Threshold *option except that it is based on colour. All continuous tones are reduced to solid colours. The number entered in the* Levels *box represents the number of colours to which your image will be reduced. If you want to explore the other commands in the* Image>**Adjustments** *menu, then feel free. You may find other procedures that could be useful.*

A filter simply changes digital information from one form to another. In practical terms, filters provide you with a range of applications that work on your image to modify it in some way. Most of these could be referred to as 'special effects', although this cinematic term is, perhaps, a little misleading. Some filters make heavy demands on your system resources in two ways. Firstly, when you load Photoshop they are loaded into the memory (RAM) of your computer. Potentially they can reduce the speed of your system significantly. To some extent this problem can be overcome by moving some of the filters that you will never, or hardly ever, use into another folder. Don't delete them, but transfer them from the Plug-Ins folder to a holding folder. When you launch Photoshop, they won't be loaded into memory. You can replace them at any time afterward if you find that you need to use them. Secondly, some filters take a long time to complete. This is dependent upon the size, resolution, and colour depth of your image and also on the raw processing speed of your computer. If you have a less than optimum machine, you may find that the use of some filters is impractical.

APPLYING EFFECTS TO CA

Filters: what's on offer

A

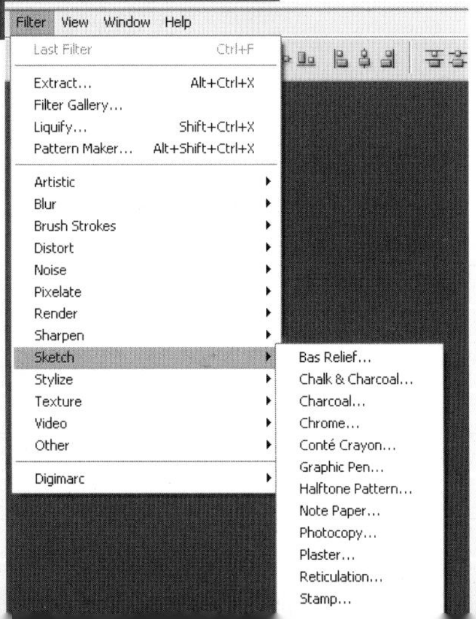

B

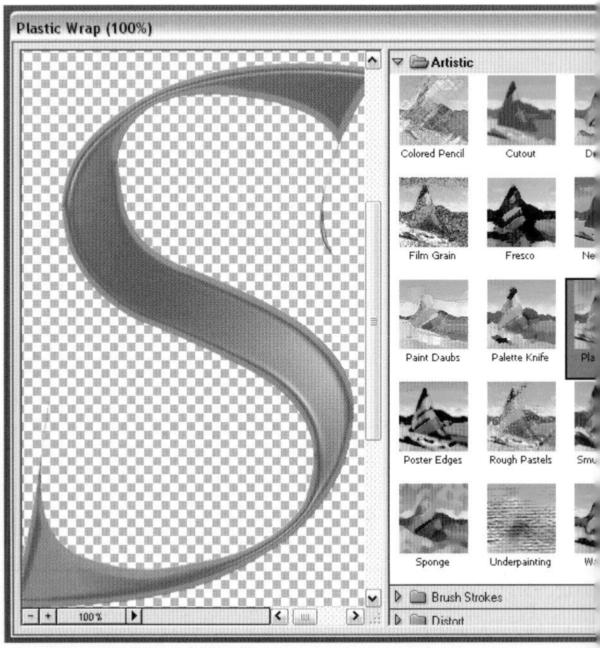

C

The Photoshop drop-down menu lists 13 main filter groups, plus a few others that we won't consider here. Each of these has a range of filters, 99 in total. The best way to find out what each of these will do is to try them. Many will be of little use for calligraphy, some will be useful for providing effects on backgrounds or on complex calligraphic images, while others can be used effectively on the calligraphy itself.

The filter groups can be selected from the drop-down menus and the filter itself selected from the submenu from which the filter options can be set. When you select certain filter groups (*Artistic, Distort, Sketch, Stylize,* or *Texture*) you are provided with a graphic interface in which you can select the filter and see a representation of the effect in a thumbnail together with a preview of the effect on your design. However, you can also access the graphic interface by selecting the *Filter Gallery* (*Filter>***Filter Gallery***). Here you can set options. For example, if you choose *Dry Brush*, you can set the *Brush Size, Brush Detail,* and *Texture.* Note also that within this box you can display a range of filters from a drop-down menu, without first having to select a filter group. Not all filters are included, however. Other filter groups display only an option box.

It is worth noting that filters can be applied to selected areas. So, if you make a selection with the *Marquee* tool, the filter effect will apply only to the selected area. Similarly, and perhaps more usefully, you can select an area using the *Magic Wand* tool. If no selection is made, the filter is applied to the whole image. Note too that type has to be rasterized before a filter will work (*Layer>Rasterize>***Type**).

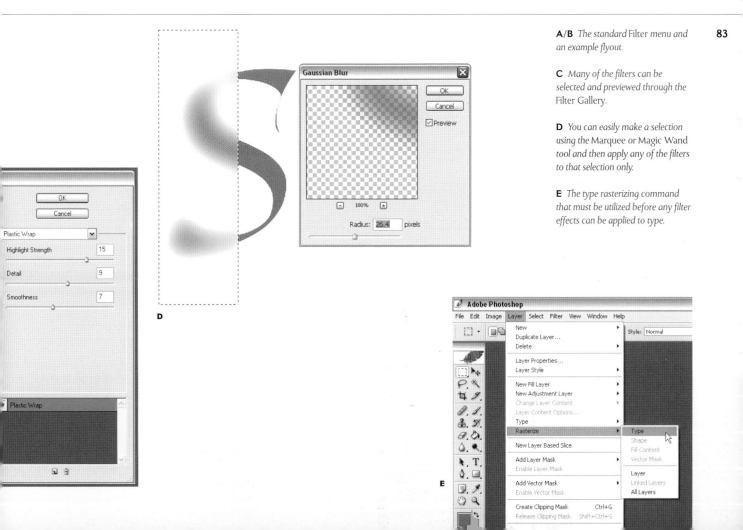

A/B *The standard* Filter *menu and an example flyout.*

C *Many of the filters can be selected and previewed through the* Filter Gallery.

D *You can easily make a selection using the* Marquee *or* Magic Wand *tool and then apply any of the filters to that selection only.*

E *The type rasterizing command that must be utilized before any filter effects can be applied to type.*

Experiment with Photoshop's filters and note the ones that you think could be useful. In this section a selected few of the filters that can effectively be applied to calligraphic lettering, as well as type, will be explored. Begin by writing one or more letters in any colour. Set the background to white. When you have worked through each example with a single letter, try applying the filters a second time to a calligraphic word – the effects may be slightly different. Use a single flat colour, not black, as some of the filters will not be effective in monochrome. Some will not work in 16-bit mode.

APPLYING EFFECTS TO CA

Filters applied to calligraphy

84

A Artistic>Colored Pencil
By adjusting the Pencil Width, Stroke Pressure, and Paper Brightness the letters are outlined in a slightly textured manner, provided the letters are large enough. This doesn't work well with small or very large lettering.

B Sketch>Photocopy
This also produces outline lettering. If the Detail and Darkness settings are roughly in the middle, the outline is medium thickness with a fade toward the centre of the letter line. Setting Detail to minimum (1) and Darkness to maximum (50) outlines the lettering in a fine, sharp line. Detail and Darkness both have to be set very low to work with lettering of a small size.

C Blur>Gaussian Blur
The most effective filter to soften the edges of your calligraphy is the Gaussian Blur. The degree to which the edges of the shapes are blurred is very controllable, from slight softening through to changing your lettering to an unintelligible blob.

A

B

C

D Artistic>Rough Pastels

You can use several different filters to make sharp-edged calligraphy look as if it was written on paper with a more or less textured surface. If you use Rough Pastels, set Light to an angle (e.g. Top Right), otherwise the effect is rather geometric.

E Stylize>Diffuse

This filter also gives lettering a rough edge, although there is no control over the degree. Set the Mode to Darken for the best effect.

F Brush Strokes>Spatter

This is probably the best filter to make your calligraphy look like 'real writing on paper'. Try adjusting Spray Radius and Smoothness to see how much control you have over the effect.

G Distort>Diffuse Glow

For a rather nice soft edge of a different sort, try using this filter. The settings will have to be very low for small lettering.

H Sketch>Bas Relief

*If you want to create three-dimensional lettering this filter will let you select the height/depth and the angle of the light. The effect is similar, but not identical, to that produced by the Stylize>**Emboss** command.*

D

E

F

G

H

J

K

I

L

I Artistic>Plastic Wrap

*In spite of its name, the effect of this filter is rather attractive when used on calligraphy. It produces three-dimensional lettering similar to that with Sketch>**Bas Relief**, but with the addition of an outline.*

J Stylize>Emboss

*This is the classic embossing filter. It differs from the Sketch>**Bas Relief** filter in that you lose the original lettering colour. For that reason it is, arguably, less useful for calligraphy.*

K Sketch>Chrome

If you really want to go wild and use your basic, simple calligraphy shapes to create further calligraphic forms, this one will do just that.

L Blur>Radial Blur

Minor distortions with this filter can be achieved when it is set to Spin and the Amount is set to a maximum of 25 (depending on the size of your lettering). For a really wild, abstract experience try setting Amount to 50.

An image, whether it is a photograph, a drawing, a design, or a piece of calligraphy, is a single integral unit, comprising all its constituent elements. Each of these elements is as important as every other, no matter how simple it is. If a superb piece of complex calligraphy is set against a flat colour background and that colour is unsuitable, it destroys the design. In a sense, it is misleading to consider backgrounds in isolation. However, more often than not, a calligraphic design will comprise one or more areas of lettering, perhaps with some design elements, all set against a background colour or colours.

Contrast, colour, tone, and content all have to be considered when deciding on backgrounds. Each of these will be considered here in turn. Colour and tone together produce the contrast between visual elements. Consider them together in your calligraphy.

Both black and white should be included as part of your colour palette and you shouldn't feel that you have to use a range of colours from Photoshop's palette. If you choose to go down the colour route, consider the effect that you want to produce. Do you want your calligraphy to be dominant on a simple unobtrusive background?

Backgrounds: basic principles

A *Complementary colours create a vibrant, often disturbing visual effect.*

B *A gray background will neutralize the brilliance of some reds.*

C *An unsuitable overtextured background in a similar colour and tone to the lettering can make calligraphy difficult to read.*

D *A slight change in the tone of the background can make all the difference to the legibility.*

E *This is a badly chosen background. Beware of rich, brightly coloured textured backgrounds that clash with the lettering.*

F *Simple, subtle backgrounds often show off calligraphy to best effect.*

Do you want to create a vibrant visual effect with strongly contrasting colours? Or do you want your lettering to merge subtly into its surroundings? The greatest contrast is between complementary colours, that is the opposite colours in the subtractive spectrum. These are the colours we see in real world objects, paintings, print etc., and not the additive model that we discussed earlier. However, colour primaries together can be very disturbing to the eye, hence the expression 'red and green should never be seen'. Note also that grey will subdue and even destroy the effect of a brilliant red.

Tone, that is the lightness or darkness of a colour, reduces the contrast between otherwise contrasting colours and can be used to reduce the overcontrasting effect of opposing colours. Using different tones is the most effective way of increasing or reducing the importance of an element in a design. Sometimes, it can be a good idea to convert your work to greyscale temporarily to see the tonal effect.

If the content of your background is a flat colour, it is a simple matter of deciding on its colour and tone. However, your calligraphy may be part of a design that includes a textured background or even one with an image. 'Soft-edged' backgrounds such as clouds, washes, and so on can be effective. Beware of anything that has a strong visual texture or comprises very distinct shapes, as these will probably interfere with the legibility of your calligraphy.

E

F

There are several ways to make a background in Photoshop. In most cases use a separate layer for your background, although you may have to flatten the image to apply adjustments. You can use the default 'background layer', but here we are referring to the image background and not the layer itself. A background can be created at the start of your project so that you can place your calligraphy on it, or at a later stage.

Simple flat backgrounds can be produced in three different ways. The first of these is to set a background at the initial point when you are determining the parameters of your canvas. To do this, firstly set the background colour in the *Toolbox*. In the document set-up window (*File>**New***) under *Background Contents* choose *Background Color* from the drop-down menu. This will provide you with a canvas background of your chosen colour. Alternatively, you can choose a colour from the *Color* palette, selecting either *Color* or *Swatches*, then use the *Paint Bucket* tool to fill the canvas. Make sure that your background layer is not locked. Finally, you can make your own background using any of Photoshop's brush or shape tools.

Backgrounds: some examples

A

B

C

D

A way of making a more complex background is to use *Styles* in the *Color* palette. Simply click on the style and your background will appear. Most of the preset styles that come with Photoshop are much too contrasty or textured in their raw form. The ones that you may find useful are *Blue Glass*, *Sunspots*, and *Chiseled Sky*. Of course you can create your own style and add it to the *Color* palette.

However you create your background, you can adjust it to work best with your calligraphy. Select *Image>* **Adjustments** and then one of the pop-up options. The most useful of these to modify background colours are *Color Balance*, *Brightness/Contrast*, and *Hue/Saturation*. With each of these, sliders modify the selected aspect of the colour. Make sure that you have *Preview* checked so that you see the effect of the adjustments instantly. It is probably best to use *Brightness/Contrast* first to set the basic tonal quality of your design. If your background is still overcolourful after making these initial adjustments, you can reduce the colour content by decreasing the *Saturation* in the *Hue/Saturation* option box. In effect this takes out some of your colour. If you reduce the saturation to zero, your background will be grey with no colour whatsoever.

If after these adjustments the actual colour tint of the background is still not to your liking, you can modify it by several means, the simplest of which is by using *Image>Adjustments>***Color Balance**. Here you will be working with the combination of cyan, red, magenta, green, yellow, and blue, but the best way to use this adjustment method is simply trial and error and forget colour theory at this point!

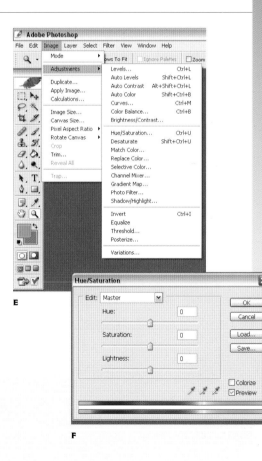

A *The* New *dialog box, showing the* Background Contents *drop-down.*

B *Photoshop's default* Blue Glass *from the* Style *palette.*

C Sunspots, *another default style from the* Style *palette.*

D Chiseled Sky *from the* Style *palette is a simple graduated fill background. The colours can be changed using one of several adjustment commands.*

E *The* Adjustments *menu, showing the available colour commands.*

F *Trial and error is the best way to make slight adjustments to the colour balance of the background.*

G *Calligraphy making effective use of simple tonal differences between the background and lettering.*

Traditionally, creating drop shadows on lettering was a highly skilled job that took a very long time. Consequently, they were not used very often in hand-rendered lettering. Programs such as Photoshop have made this process easy and instant. Adding drop shadows to your calligraphy can produce a 3D effect, making your lettering stand out from the background. It sounds easy – and it is. You will find a whole range of options that affect how your drop shadow will look, including colour, opacity, size etc. Make sure that the lettering to which you apply the effects is on an independent layer or it won't work.

Drop shadows and other layer effects are accessed by clicking on the *Add Layer Style* icon at the bottom of the *Layers* palette. When you select one effect, a box appears that lets you select any of the layer effects, not just the one you have selected. You will probably be impressed by what some of these effects can do to your calligraphy. Try them on single letters and on words, sentences, or paragraphs. Beware: don't let your work become overstylized!

It is best to illustrate the layer effects by examples. These are the ones you will find most useful. Each of the layer effects can be combined with every other.

Drop shadows and other layer effects

APPLYING EFFECTS TO CA

90

DROP SHADOW
If you set the Size to zero you will get a copy of your lettering, irrespective of any other setting. For a true drop shadow effect set Size to something greater than zero. Select the shadow colour and the Distance before you make adjustments to the other parameters. If you set the Distance to zero you can place a soft-edge shadow evenly around your calligraphy. This can be very effective. For a very 'normal-looking' drop shadow apply it to the lower right of the lettering, as if the light were coming from the upper left, not too far from it, with some overlap, and without an exaggerated soft edge.

OUTER GLOW
This creates a similar effect to setting the Distance of the Drop Shadow to zero. However, you can get some really wild effects by selecting one of the Gradients.

BEVEL AND EMBOSS
*This is a much better way to create three-dimensional calligraphy than using either the Stylize>**Emboss** or Stylize> **Bas Relief** commands. With this option you have much greater control over the effect.*

GRADIENT OVERLAY
This is an easy way to make a simple gradient over the lettering. You have control over many parameters including colour, angle, and style.

STROKE
Stroke is the best way to apply an outline to the lettering. Among other things, you can choose the colour, width, and style.

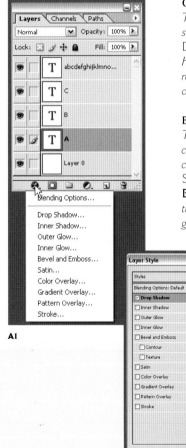

A1

A2

A *The Layer Style option window lets you select the layer style and set its parameters. Note that the layers can be combined with each other.*

B *Setting the drop shadow Size to zero will give you a copy of your lettering and most of the other settings will have no effect.*

C *Set the Distance to zero to create a soft-edge surround to the lettering.*

D *A realistic-looking drop shadow should not be too far from the lettering. The distance shown in this illustration is about right.*

E *Outer Glow can produce some dramatic effects if you use Gradients from the option box.*

F *Layer Style is probably the best way to convert your lettering to 3D.*

G *Layer Style is one of several ways you can apply gradients in Photoshop.*

H *Stroke is a good way to apply an outline to shapes. The subtle controls make it an effective method of giving your calligraphy an outline.*

I *All the Layer Styles can be used together, though not necessarily with a desirable effect. Here several of the styles have been applied to the large and small letters.*

B

C

D

E

F

G

H

I

Every bitmap graphics application will let you fill shapes, almost invariably using a tool called the Paint Bucket, or something similar. This works by clicking within a shape. When there is a distinct difference between the colour of the shape and the background, the fill colour will go only as far as the edge of the shape. But what happens if the shape is not distinct or has shaded edges? Where the fill stops is determined by the set 'tolerance'. The higher the tolerance the more the fill will spread. Some programs will let you define a selected area in some way and the fill will not extend beyond its boundary.

Fills

92

Photoshop lets you use this basic fill method and offers an alternative, the *Edit>**Fill*** command. There are different opinions on which method is the better. Some users consider the *Paint Bucket* tool as all but useless. Try the step-by-step examples here and decide which is the better for you. There are several procedures in Photoshop that relate very closely to the basic fill. Some have been covered earlier and others will be explored later.

You may not use basic fills very often in your calligraphy. They are probably more useful when working with graphic shapes. Arguably, other methods of changing the colour and pattern of foreground lettering and its background are more flexible and offer greater creative potential.

words

1

1 *Open a new document and create a layer in addition to the background. Using a calligraphic brush, write a letter or two in a colour that is clearly different from the background. You will use this for each of these steps.*

2 *The basic fill using the Paint Bucket tool will be explored first. Note that when you select the tool, the options are displayed on the main menu bar, and that you can fill with either the foreground colour or a pattern. Change the foreground colour and, using the Paint Bucket tool, click on your lettering, ensuring that your letter layer is active. If the lines of your letters are continuous, they will all be filled. If not, a second or third click may be necessary. Use the Edit>**Step Backward** command to return to your unfilled lettering.*

2b

2a

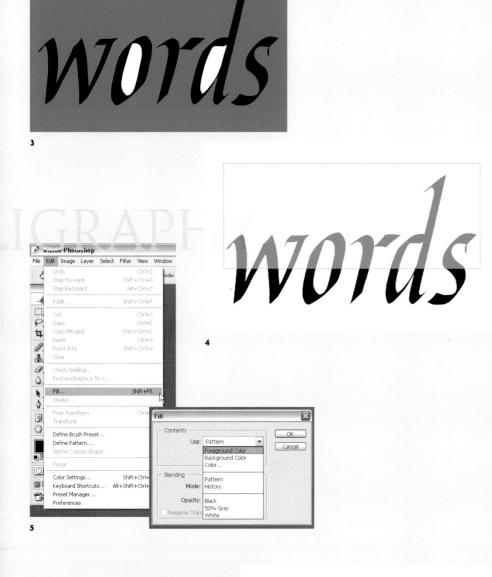

3 *Select the background with the* Magic Wand *tool. Using the* Paint Bucket *tool again, click on the background. Note that the counters of letters will not be filled and will have to be selected and clicked again. Step backward to the initial letters.*

4 *Using the* Rectangular Marquee *tool select the top half of your lettering. Using the* Paint Bucket *tool click on the parts of the lettering within the marquee. Only that part will be filled. Instead of using the marquee selection, you could have used the* Magic Wand *tool to select the lettering. Step backward.*

5 *Select* Edit>**Fill** *from the main drop-down menu. Now you will see that you have a wider range of options, including filling with the foreground colour, the background colour, another colour or a pattern. Select one of these options and click OK. You will see that the whole canvas is filled with the colour or pattern of your choice because you haven't selected an area. Undo or step backward.*

6 *Using the* Magic Wand *tool, select your lettering. Repeat step 5. This time only your lettering will be filled. One final option: if you apply* Edit>**Fade Fill** *you can easily adjust its* Opacity. *However, this doesn't work with some pattern fills.*

Gradient fills can be used in digital
to create a range of different effe
simplest, a gradient fill used with
can add interest to a single letter or a bloc
example, straight black calligraphy can be
by introducing slight changes from black t
over the whole text area. It can also be use
the varying opacity of coloured ink or pigr
traditional hand-rendered calligraphy. Grad
be made up of any number of colours, pro
there are at least two. In an extreme form,

APPLYING EFFECTS TO

Gradient fills

94   **MAKING THE GRADIENTS**

1 *Create a single one-colour letter with the* Brush *tool – black will be fine. Make a vector path and adjust the form as necessary.*

2 *Select the* Gradient *tool. You will see a range of gradient options in the toolbar.*

3 *Clicking on the* Gradient Picker *will reveal the gradient presets.*

4 *Clicking in the actual gradient pattern in the toolbar will bring up the* Gradient Editor. *In the* Editor *you can select colours and the number of colours. Clicking anywhere above or below the gradient bar will add another colour to the gradient. Double-clicking brings up the* Color Picker. *The sliders adjust the location of colours.*

5 *Draggi the lette chosen grad direction yo want to wo for this proc Try some fu*

available in the Styles palette, which will be described later, include some complex gradients that can be applied very easily to calligraphy.

The simplest gradient fill is the Linear gradient, which fills a shape with colour that changes from one to another. This change can be in any direction – from top to bottom, bottom to top, left to right, or right to left. The gradient can also be angled so that the change takes place from, say, top left to bottom right. Other types of gradient are Radial, Reflected, and Diamond, which are less effective when used with lettering but are worth experimenting with.

As with many of its procedures, Photoshop offers a large number of different ways to create and apply the effects. The examples shown here will give you the opportunity to try out some of the basic effects and apply them to calligraphic letters. Note that gradient fills can be effective when applied to the letters or to the background. Be careful, however, with the use of colours that are too light and that can end up making your lettering difficult to read. Also, do not be tempted to use too many colours in a gradient fill, since this can become visually confusing.

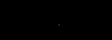

A *A simple fill applied right to left.*

B *An angled fill in three tones of the same colour. Set these in the Gradient Editor.*

C *A similar fill, this time vertical, top to bottom at an angle. Holding Shift while dragging constrains the fill to 45-degree increments.*

D *A gradient fill applied to the background, leaving the letter in a uniform colour.*

E *A Linear gradient has been applied top to bottom in the background and bottom to top in the counters of the letter.*

Styles are really presets of the layer styles that we looked at earlier. They are located in the *Styles* palette. If your calligraphy is on an independent layer, you simply click on the preset style and this will be applied to your lettering. The basic range that is displayed in the *Styles* palette by default looks pretty limited. This is deceptive. Click on the palette menu button and a vast range of style options is offered. Many of these look like variants of the default set – emboss with drop shadow or gradient filled. But, perhaps not surprisingly, the ones under *Text Effects* and *Text Effects 2* will probably excite you most.

From a design perspective, most Photoshop preset styles are more suited to a commercial application of lettering, such as logos, and may lack the subtlety and sensitivity of calligraphy as an art form. However, if the effects are selected carefully and modifications made to them as described in the next section, they can be useful for a wide range of applications. Illustrated here is a selection of what may be the most useful ones.

APPLYING EFFECTS TO CA

Styles

A *Blue Gradient with Stroke*

B *Brushed metal*

C *Chrome – Fat*

D *Clear with Heavy Stroke*

E *Clear Double Black Stroke*

F *Green Gradient with Stroke*

G *Liquid Rainbow*

H *Clear Emboss*

I *Satin*

J *Shaded Red Bevel*

K *Fat Black and White*

You will have realized by now that you are not restricted to the style gallery that is supplied with Photoshop. An infinite range of styles can be created, either by designing them from scratch using the *Styles* palette or by modifying one of those supplied. After experimenting for a long time, finding one or more that you particularly like and could find useful in future, you don't want to have to go through the procedure of setting it up again. Photoshop lets you name the style and add it to the *Styles* palette. This section on styles will be completed with a worked example that uses some of the techniques described earlier and shows you how styles can be saved for future use.

APPLYING EFFECTS TO CA

Creating styles

98

1

2

3

1 *Create a new document.*
Set the foreground to black and the background to white. Using a calligraphic brush, write a word freely – any word will do. Alternatively, you can import a calligraphic word from another program. Ensure that the lettering is on a discrete layer from the background.

2 *We will now add a* Layer Style. *Click on the* Layer Style *icon at the bottom of the* Layers *palette and select* Drop Shadow. *The* Layers *dialog box will be displayed with the options for* Drop Shadow *selected. Set the* Blend Mode *to* Normal, Opacity *to 80,* Size *to 250, and all other parameters to zero. Choose a colour other than black. This will produce a soft glow around the word.*

3 *Select* Inner Glow *from the* Layer Style *dialog. Set* Opacity *to 75,* Size *to 35, and other settings to zero.*

4 *Choose* Bevel and Emboss. *Set* Style *to* Pillow Emboss, Technique *to* Smooth, Depth *to 970%,* Size *to 54, and choose a colour.*

5 *The style that you have created can now be saved for later use. There are three ways of doing this. You can click the* New Style *icon in the* Layer Style *dialog box, drag and drop the layer that holds the style information, or you can simply click on the* Styles *palette (the cursor will change to a paint bucket). These three methods will bring up a dialog box in which you can name your new style. Use whichever method you find convenient and name your new style.*

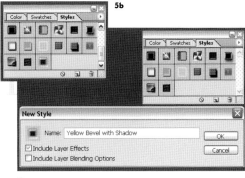

5b

5a

6 *We will now make sure that your style really has been saved. Open a new document and draw a small squiggle with the* Paint Brush *tool on an independent layer. Click on the icon for the new style that you have designed. The style should appear applied to your squiggle. Close this temporary document.*

7 *So far, styles have been used on the actual calligraphy and not on the surrounding background. Applying style to the background can produce interesting and sometimes unexpected effects. Select your background layer and make sure it isn't locked. Increase the* Spread *of the drop shadow to 50 then try applying different styles to this layer. You will find that many don't work very well but others will produce quite spectacular effects.*

7

Large areas of calligraphy or type matter have a visual texture that is subtly but noticeably affected by the letterform, letter spacing, and line spacing. Some lettering styles are 'quiet' and very easy on the eye. Some are rich and very busy in effect. As you are more likely to be using Photoshop for small amounts of calligraphic text, perhaps a word or two, this sort of visual texture will not be as important as would be the case with paragraphs. You may wish to give the matter of visual texture some consideration when using typefaces with your calligraphy, however.

Texturizing lettering has to be done with great restraint so that the letterforms are not destroyed in the process. Caution has already been suggested in using highly textured backgrounds that can make calligraphy illegible if used unwisely. Textured backgrounds can be used to simulate different paper surfaces. If your calligraphy is 'virtual' and is to be viewed only on a computer screen, creating these paperlike backgrounds is aesthetically valid. If your calligraphy is to be printed, possibly on an inkjet printer, it could be argued that you would be better printing on the actual paper, rather than using what may

Texture

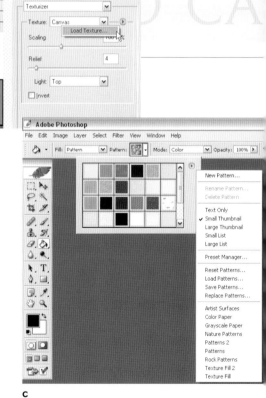

B

A

Large areas of calligraphy or type matter have a visual texture that is subtly but noticeably affected by the letterform, letter spacing and line spacing. Some lettering styles are 'quiet' and very easy on the eye. Some are rich and very busy in effect.

Large areas of calligraphy or type matter have a visual texture that is subtly but noticeably affected by the letterform, letter spacing and line spacing. Some lettering styles are 'quiet' and very easy on the eye. Some are rich and very busy in effect.

C

A *Two different typefaces illustrating the varied textures that already exist in type.*

B *The default textures available in the Filter Gallery.*

C *The pattern menu available from the tool bar with the Paint Bucket tool selected.*

be a poor substitute for it. However, textured paperlike backgrounds can be used creatively even in these situations. For example, imagine printing a paperlike texture on a quite different paper surface.

Photoshop's basic *Filter Gallery* (select *Filter*>**Texture** or *Filter*>**Filter Gallery**) is limited to only six patterns: *Craquelure, Grain, Mosaic Tiles, Patchwork, Stained Glass,* and *Texturizer.* This last one gives you access to several more stored in the Preset/Texture and Preset/Patterns/Adobe ImageReady Only folders. Another and possibly better solution is to use a pattern fill with adjustments to colour, brightness, or contrast as necessary. Only some of the preset patterns make suitable calligraphic 'surfaces' and some of those need to have the brightness, contrast, and/or opacity reduced considerably. With the *Paint Bucket* tool highlighted,

selecting *Fill*>**Patterns** and clicking on the pop-up menu lets you choose a pattern fill group. The ones that will produce the best background for calligraphy include *Artistic Surfaces* (*Dark Coarse Weave* and *Stone,* both of which are greyscale), *Color Paper* (many good ones), *Patterns 2,* and some in *Texture Fill 2* (greyscale). Many others have a very regular visual texture that looks rather artificial.

Yet another option is to make your own pattern by calling up *Filter*>**Pattern Maker** from the main menu. From any image on a layer you can select a section and click *Generate.* As the pattern is generated by repeating the selected part of the image, the result is usually very geometric. If you want to create a paperlike effect you will have to begin with a very fuzzy or grainy selection and experiment with the various parameters.

D

E

F

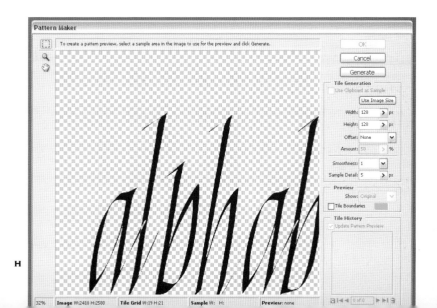

G

D *A background texture applied using the* Dark Coarse Weave *pattern from the* Artistic Surfaces *palette.* Opacity *was set to 40% and adjustments made to the colour. Note that the texture appears through the lettering.*

E *The background pattern here is* Buff Textured, *one of the many good patterns in the* Color Paper *palette.*

F *The basic* Denim *pattern in the* Patterns 2 *palette has had the* Opacity *reduced to 70% in this example to give a more subtle effect.*

G *This background texture is* Weave 5 *from the* Texture Fill 2 *palette.*

H *The* Pattern Maker *dialog ready to generate a new pattern.*

H

We are entering the danger zone! Most of the Photoshop effects that we have examined so far have been produced through what are termed 'corrective filters' that leave your basic image intact and adjust such things as colour, tone, edges, and so on. Here we look at what you can do to alter or convert your calligraphy from a simple word or words to more or less graphic images that may sometimes retain little resemblance to your original work. The procedures used for these effects are called 'destructive filters', for obvious reasons – therein lies the danger.

Special effects

102

Always ask yourself what you are trying to achieve with your calligraphy – legibility, visual effect, or both. The degree to which these filters will distort your original letterforms can usually be controlled by the settings within the option. This can be previewed and either accepted or rejected.

Most of the filters that will produce the special effects of the sort that we will look at here can be found either in the *Filter Gallery* or by selecting *Filter>**Distort*** from the main menu bar. You may also find some useful effects under *Filter>**Pixelate*** and *Filter>Render>**Lighting Effects***. Explore these at your leisure.

One way in which abstract calligraphic images can be used is by combining them with the main legible text of your design. In this way they can form an effective backdrop to text. Don't forget the basic principles that we have established regarding the potential conflict between a rich, textural background and the main calligraphy.

The first group of examples illustrates some special effects created by using selections from the *Filter Gallery* and by using *Filter>**Distort***. The second group overleaf shows how more than one filter effect can be applied to a single image and also how calligraphy that has been distorted until it is little more than an abstract design can be used with legible lettering as an element in the design.

A

B

C

D

E

F

G

H

A Filter>Distort>**Pinch** *is the same as* Pinch/Punch *in other programs. It distorts the image by 'pulling' or 'pushing' it from the center.*

B *The rotation of the* Filter> Distort>**Twirl** *effect can be controlled so that only slight distortion is applied. Applying more rotation creates an abstract calligraphic form.*

C Filter>Distort>**Wave** *creates a zigzag effect. As with* Twirl, *the degree of distortion can be controlled.*

D Filter>Pixelate>**Mosaic** *applies a pattern of pixels of a chosen size of the image.*

E *The* Coloured Pencil *option from the* Artistic *filters doesn't distort the lettering if the parameters are selected carefully. Some interesting effects can be created with this filter.*

F *A simple application of* Glowing Edges *from the* Artistic *group of filters tends to eat away at the edges of the lettering.*

G *Another* Artistic *filter,* Stained Glass, *applies an irregular honeycomb pattern to the selection or layer.*

H Filter>Distort>**ZigZag** *with the* Pond Ripples *option selected produces an effect similar to applying both the* Wave *and* Twirl *filters simultaneously.*

103

A

These are just a few of the effects that you may find useful in your calligraphy. Explore Photoshop fully and find out what you like and what you don't like. Try out the examples for yourself, then vary some of the steps to get a different effect. Keep a note of the procedures that you follow. It is very easy to find yourself in the situation where you have achieved a spectacular result but don't remember how you got there. Photoshop's *History* palette will help you keep a track of what you have applied but don't rely on it entirely.

APPLYING EFFECTS TO CA

Special effects: some examples

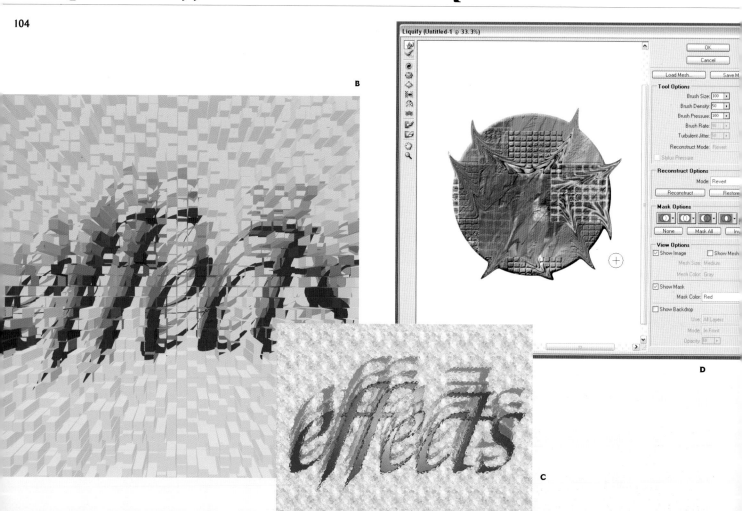

B

D

C

A *A simple repeat of the word 'effects' in different tones of the same colour on a textured background. This, or elements from it, has been used in all the effects examples.*

B Filter>Stylize>**Extrude** *was applied to the basic image. The effect is interesting but may have limited applications to calligraphy.*

C *In this example, two filters were applied to the lettering,* Plastic Wrap *then* Diffuse Glow. *The image was then flattened and the* Filter> Distort>**Glass** *effect was used.*

D *The* Liquefy *filter (*Filter>**Liquefy***) lets you pull parts of your image as if it were made from a stiff syrup.*

E *This image will be used in the following example as a background. The* Wave *filter was first applied to the word 'effects'. This was then greatly softened using the* Filter>Blur> **Gaussian Blur** *command.* Noise *was then added (*Filter>**Noise***). Numerous strokes with the* Liquefy *filter were applied evenly across the design, and the contrast was reduced to make the pattern less dominant.*

F *Crisp lettering that contrasts with the softness of the background was applied to the image created above.*

G *The lettering was kept on as a separate layer. The* Twirl *effect was again applied to it to create a crisp, linear design over the soft-edged background shape.*

H *To complete the design, the word 'calligraphic' was added. If you work through this example, you can either write the lettering with a calligraphic brush or use a calligraphic typeface, fitting the text to a predrawn path as was demonstrated earlier in the book.*

The terms 'composition', 'layout', and 'design' are, to some extent, interchangeable although their meanings are slightly different. 'Composition' tends to be used in the context of art or photography and refers to the arrangement of elements in a picture. 'Layout' is the term used by designers for the way in which type, illustrations, and perhaps other objects are positioned on a page. We can use the term 'design' for both composition and layout. The word has a not-so-obvious meaning. When we consider how the lettering in a piece of calligraphy should be arranged on the page (or canvas in the terminology of Photoshop) we are designing, and the end product has been designed. In other words, a design is the result of a carefully worked-out plan.

In design there are rules. There are also rules that can be broken. There would be no such thing as creativity if all art and design were governed by rules. However, an understanding of some basic design principles is important to produce good calligraphic work. In a different context we have already examined the design of letters and words and emphasized the importance of good letterform and spacing. Here we are considering how several elements –

Composition, layout, and design

A

A One design approach is to position elements visually to create balance or effect. In this design a number of capital 'As' of different sizes and with different filters applied are arranged in a simple balanced design.

B If a page or canvas is clearly divided into two sections, the classic proportion of each is called the golden mean. In this illustration the image is divided into two horizontally. The proportion of A to B is the same as B to the total canvas height.

C Try to avoid using lettering styles that are so similar that it will look like a mistake.

D Use lettering styles that are either the same or, as in this case, very different from each other.

individual calligraphic letters, words, or small groups of words – can be arranged interestingly on the canvas. Since Photoshop is not the best tool to produce more than a few words, any large area of continuous text is likely to be typographic rather than calligraphic. The topic of calligraphy and type is tackled elsewhere in the book.

There are two basic ways of arranging elements within a shape. One is simply to position everything where it looks 'right', so that the whole design looks as if it has been considered and nothing looks out of place. The shape, scale, colour, tone, and position of each element have to be considered. This is the most difficult way of designing and depends on the sensitivity of the designer or calligrapher. When the design works well it can be lively and dynamic. When it doesn't it can be an embarrassment! There are ways to analyze a design that can help to resolve problems. Artists have been aware of the 'golden mean' or 'golden section' for centuries. This principle suggests that, when a canvas is divided visually into two parts, the proportion of the smaller part to the larger part should be the same as the proportion of the larger part to the whole canvas. In practice, we don't measure this but can quickly develop an eye for what's right. Another sound principle is not to use very similar letterforms together, as it will look like a mistake. Use contrast in your design. This can also apply to colour. Remember that, no matter how good the calligraphy, your creation won't succeed if the overall design is unsatisfactory.

ELEMENTS

A

B golden mean

C

D

A very freeform type layout or design may well be appropriate and effective under certain circumstances. Often, however, you will want to arrange your lettering in a fairly formal and more rigid manner. This brings us to the second approach to a calligraphic design. When a designer faces the problem of having to arrange large amounts of complex text, such as the text in this book, it would be very difficult to produce acceptable page designs if each one were tackled in a very freeform way and simply relied on the designer's visual judgment to make them work.

Typographic designers use grids to help them position text and illustration and, in the case of multi-page design, to help them produce a design in which each page relates in some way to every other. By using grids it is much easier to locate text and illustration within the page or canvas in a way that looks ordered and consistent.

We saw earlier how you can create and modify guides in Photoshop by dragging them from the horizontal and vertical rulers that you have enabled using *View>**Rulers***. These guides can be used to create a working grid to help with layout, as seen in this step-by-step example.

Working with grids

108

1 *Start a new document. Make sure that you have the horizontal and vertical rulers displayed.*

2 *Drag four horizontal rulers and four vertical rulers onto your page. They don't have to be in exactly the same position as in the illustration but make the space between the second and third guides quite small in the case of both verticals and horizontals.*

3 *For convenience, we will use type to create the elements that will be used in this design. Type some text into the lower right rectangle of the grid. Make sure it fits exactly. On another type layer type 'rids' as part of the word 'Grids' and make it fit the right rectangle of the grid. Use a different typeface if you wish.*

rids

A very free layout or design may well be appropriate in some circumstances. Often, however, you will want to arrange your lettering in the fairly formal way. This brings us to the second approach to a calligraphic design. When a designer has the problem of arranging large amounts of complex text, like the text in this book, it would be very difficult to produce acceptable page designs if each one was tackled in a very free way and simply relying on visual judgement. Typographic designers use grids to help them position text and illustration and, in the case of multi-page design, to help them produce a design in which each page relates in some way to every other. By using grids it is much easier to locate text and illustration within the page or canvas in a way that looks as if it was done as a conscious decision.

4 On another layer type the capital letter 'G' to complete the word 'Grids'. Fit this exactly to the top left rectangle. You will see that everything works well together. Each element relates to the others visually, even though they are of very different sizes. However, the design is rather formal and lacks vitality.

5 This is where we break the rules. Replace the letter 'G' with one from a different typeface, ideally one from a script typeface, if you have one installed. Let it extend beyond the grid in any direction you want. You can even make it overlap the rest of the word or the text block. By breaking through the grid we have added more interest without destroying the structure of the design. Use this procedure sparingly. Try moving the elements of the design around to see what happens if you ignore the grid. Also try applying some filter effects to see how a well-structured layout permits quite dramatic changes to the lettering.

4

Grids

A very free layout or design may well be appropriate in some circumstances. Often, however, you will want to arrange your lettering in the fairly formal way. This brings us to the second approach to a calligraphic design. When a designer has the problem of arranging large amounts of complex text, like the text in this book, it would be very difficult to produce acceptable page designs if each one was tackled in a very free way and simply relying on visual judgement. Typographic designers use grids to help them position text and illustration and, in the case of multi-page design, to help them produce a design in which each page relates in some way to every other. By using grids it is much easier to locate text and illustration within the page or canvas in a way that looks as if it was done as a conscious decision.

5

Grids

A very free layout or design may well be appropriate in some circumstances. Often, however, you will want to arrange your lettering in the fairly formal way. This brings us to the second approach to a calligraphic design. When a designer has the problem of arranging large amounts of complex text, like the text in this book, it would be very difficult to produce acceptable page designs if each one was tackled in a very free way and simply relying on visual judgement. Typographic designers use grids to help them position text and illustration and, in the case of multi-page design, to help them produce a design in which each page relates in some way to every other. By using grids it is much easier to locate text and illustration within the page or canvas in a way that looks as if it was done as a conscious decision.

Grids

A very free layout or design may well be appropriate in some circumstances. Often, however, you will want to arrange your lettering in the fairly formal way. This brings us to the second approach to a calligraphic design. When a designer has the problem of arranging large amounts of complex text, like the text in this book, it would be very difficult to produce acceptable page designs if each one was tackled in a very free way and simply relying on visual judgement. Typographic

Once you have mastered the art of calligraphy and found how Photoshop can create effects through the range of techniques that have been described so far, you may wonder whether there could possibly be anything else that can be used to develop your creative ideas even further. Indeed there is. So far we have worked with designs that are, in effect, a single layer. They may have been created using Photoshop's multilayer methodology but, ultimately, when all of the layers are flattened, the design doesn't change. What then if we can take two or more designs or parts of

designs and control how they interact with each other? Of course, we can place one image over another and control the transparency of the upper layer, but the effect is to weaken the transparent layer while the lower layer remains intact. Make the lower layer more transparent and the whole image becomes rather insipid. There could be occasions when you may wish to use transparency in this way, but we really want more control over the way that Photoshop's layers can interact. This can be done through the blending options. To demonstrate the principles we will use two calligraphic words, one straight

WORKING W

Complex overlays

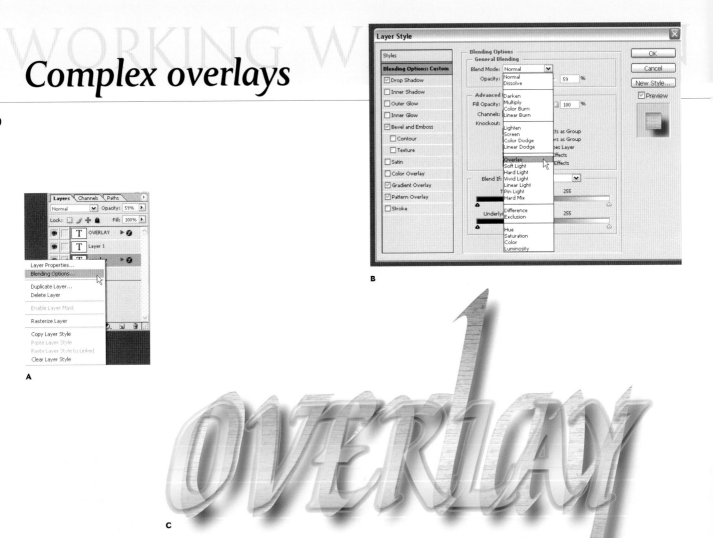

A

B

C

over the top of the other, to which different filters have been applied. You can decide how this effect could be applied to your lettering.

There are several ways you can display the blending options. One of the simplest is to right-click (Control-click on a Mac) on the overlay layer in the *Layers* palette and select *Blending Options*. You will be presented with a perplexing array of blending settings within the *Layer Style* window. Here we will explore one. You can experiment with the others later to see if they may be useful.

When two images are on separate layers in a document make sure that the image you want to overlay on the other is hierarchically above it. Right-click on the overlay layer and select *Blending Options*. This will display the *Blending Options* dialog box. The *Blend Mode* drop-

down menu will offer 22 different methods. It is a good idea to select *Overlay* first to see the effect. It may be that you will rarely need to use the others with calligraphy. However, the effect can be very strong. Reducing the opacity within the *Blending Options* box can tone down the overlay. If you have *Preview* checked, you can monitor the effect of adjusting the blending parameters.

From a design perspective, some of the principles that have already been explored in the book should be remembered. When you use overlays you are combining the characteristics of both images. In many instances, if the two elements are combined on a 50/50 basis, then the effect will be too complex visually and you will have to adjust one or other of the images so that it then becomes the dominant one.

D

A *The* Blending Options *command can be found by right-clicking on a layer in the* Layers *palette.*

B *The* Blending Options *dialog allows you to control the* Blend Mode *to a greater degree than is possible through the* Layers *palette.*

C *Blending two layers with the Overlay option can combine the images in an overcomplex way, making neither of them very legible.*

D *Some adjustment to opacity, on one or both layers, can help to make the lettering on one of the layers dominant and legible.*

The following two step-by-step exercises demonstrate how to control overlays by using blending options so that designs created from several overlapping images can work effectively. In the first, two simple images are combined. In the second, several image overlays are blended. If you want a bit of adventure, you can try setting the blending options to one of the other 21 offered by Photoshop.

1 Start a new document, any size, with a white background and a resolution of 300 pixels per inch. On an independent layer, write three lines of text using a calligraphic brush. Don't be too concerned about the quality of your calligraphy for this but make sure it is rhythmic. If you prefer, and if you have the software, you can write the text in another program such as Adobe Illustrator and import it into Photoshop. Alternatively, you can import some scanned text.

2 Apply a filter effect of your choice to the lettering. Even if your writing was rather rough, you will see that the filter adds some interest to it and greatly improves the look of the calligraphy. If you have used one of the default filters, make some adjustments to it. Add an even spread drop shadow around the lettering.

3 Apply a different filter to the background layer. Flatten the image using the command Layer>**Flatten Image**. Save the image to disk.

WORKING WITH DESIGN

Overlays: step-by-step example 1

1

2

3

4

4 *Start a second document, identical in size and resolution to the first. Make the background white as before. Once again, on an independent layer, create a few lines of text. In this example, numerals have been used so that they relate to the text in the first image. For the lettering in the second document you could use a script typeface. Apply a filter and adjust it in the same way as you did with the lettering in the first document. Apply a different filter to the background layer. Flatten the image and save it.*

5 *Load both images so that they are visible together on your computer screen. Select the whole second image using the rectangular marquee and* copy it to the clipboard (Edit>**Copy**). *Make the first image active and open a new layer. Paste the second image into this layer (Edit>***Paste***). Close the second image as you won't need it any more. Make sure that Layer 0 is above Layer 1 and right-click on it. Choose Blending Options. From the Blend Mode drop-down select Overlay.*

6 *Both images will be displayed with equal weight. The result is somewhat confusing visually and we have to make adjustments. We could make either layer dominant. In this example we will make the calligraphy the main visual element. In the Layers palette, reduce the Opacity of the layer that you want to be less obvious.*

7 *We could leave the design like that but the background numerals are still a bit hard-edged. A Gaussian Blur set to a radius of 50 pixels will soften the image and greatly improve the design.*

6

7

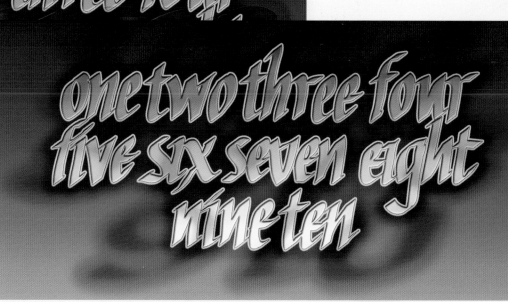

Being able to blend layers of calligraphic images as overlays in Photoshop is, arguably, more useful than the function for which this facility was designed by the application's authors. The merging of photographic layers by this method is often akin to projecting two slides at the same time to create a rather confused, though admittedly sometimes intriguing, image. In the case of calligraphic lettering, since the shapes tend to be strong and well defined from the outset, the resulting combinations are often very acceptable with or without adjustment.

Although the following exercise is worked within a single document using layers, you may find it easier to work on the separate elements of a calligraphic design in separate documents, especially if the design is complex. Each can then be copied and pasted into any other.

Overlays: step-by-step example 2

1 *Start a new document with a white background. Unlock the background to make it Layer 0. Using the Brush tool write the letter 'A' on a new layer. There is no need to create a new layer manually as a type layer will be generated whenever you start typing the letter. On separate type layers, write the letters 'B', 'C', 'D', and 'E' in either the same or different sizes. At this stage the colour doesn't matter, nor does the position. Both of these will be changed later.*

2 *Using the Ellipse tool and holding Shift to constrain the proportion to a circle, draw a coloured circle about the same size or slightly smaller than the letter 'A'. Soften the edge of the circle by using Filter>Blur>**Gaussian Blur** with Radius set to more than 90 pixels. Make sure the shape layer is above the type layer and drag the circle until it is centered under the 'A'. Set the colour of the letter to something lighter than the circle.*

3 *Repeat the process with the rest of the letters by selecting each layer in turn.*

4 *Combine each letter with its circle by using the command Layer>**Merge Visible**. In the Layers palette you will have to hide layers except the two that you are merging and make sure that one of the two layers that you are merging is active.*

1

2

3

5

6

7a

4a

Adobe Photoshop

File   Edit   Image   Layer   Select   Filter   View   Window   Help

New	▶
Duplicate Layer...	
Delete	▶
Layer Properties...	
Layer Style	▶
New Fill Layer	▶
New Adjustment Layer	▶
Change Layer Content	▶
Layer Content Options...	
Type	▶
Rasterize	▶
New Layer Based Slice	
Add Layer Mask	▶
Enable Layer Mask	
Add Vector Mask	▶
Enable Vector Mask	
Create Clipping Mask	Ctrl+G
Release Clipping Mask	Shift+Ctrl+G
Arrange	▶
Align Linked	▶
Distribute Linked	▶
Lock All Layers In Set...	
Merge Down	Ctrl+E
Merge Visible	Shift+Ctrl+E
Flatten Image	
Matting	▶

4b

5 Drag the letter/circle shapes so that they overlap each other as shown in the illustration. At this point you may wish to crop the image using the Crop tool from the Toolbox.

6 Working with each letter/circle shape in turn, blend each layer using Blending Options *and selecting* Overlay *as you did with the two-layer example. The result should be an interesting merge of shape and colour.*

7 Try using other blending options. You can experiment blending only some of the layers or all of them to see the different effects.

7b

7c

If you don't want to use any of the *Advanced Blending Options* in the *Layer Styles* palette, you can blend layers very simply by choose the blending mode from the drop-down menu in the *Layers* palette. Here too you set the opacity of the layer, as we have already seen. In effect, making adjustments to the opacity affects how much you see of the colours on the layer or layers below. In Photoshop it is easy to get very confused with the use of the term 'transparency' in the application although, strictly speaking, the term is correctly used. Photoshop uses 'transparency' in several contexts, especially in connection with the use of masks, which are beyond the scope of this book. Anything that is transparent is completely clear. Glass is the perfect example. Translucency, on the other hand, has a range of opacity from completely opaque to virtually transparent.

We have already seen the value of being able to adjust the translucency of a layer when it is blended with another to avoid visual conflict between them. There are other times when adjusting translucency is very useful. If your calligraphy is written on a simulated textured background you may wish to have that texture show

Transparency and translucency

116

A

B

C

D

through your lettering just as it would with translucent ink on a textured paper. This effect can easily be achieved by adjusting the opacity of the lettering colour. You can also simulate the pen and ink effect of overlapping strokes. With the traditional material you would get a buildup of colour resulting in the overlap area being darker. To achieve this effect you can use the *Flow* setting of the *Brush* tool. When set to a low value, say 10, this allows ink to show through as you write over it. Also, the lettering will retain its sharp edge and won't be affected by the texture of the background. This too can be adjusted to simulate writing on a rough surface, as demonstrated

earlier. However, you should ensure that the textured edge of the lettering that you apply looks realistic against the textured background in which it is written.

Using different translucencies in different parts of your calligraphy design can be a very effective tool. You could have one piece of text written with the opacity set to 50% and another set to 100% solid. Type may look better when it is opaque and could contrast very nicely with calligraphic lettering written with a very translucent colour. Sometimes you may wish to create some background lettering with the opacity set very low so that the effect is very pale and delicate.

F

E

A *The translucency of the whole layer can be set with the* Opacity *slider in the* Layers *palette.*

B *Two different colours set to 60% opacity were used in this example.*

C *When letter strokes are overlapped the colour doesn't build up in the same way as with pen and ink. The* Flow *control helps to some extent, but doesn't work in quite the same way.*

D *Another way to achieve the build up of colour on overlapped strokes is to have the strokes of the letters on different layers, as is the case here.*

E *The texture of the background doesn't affect the edge of the letters. They remain crisp and smooth.*

F *Opaque type with translucent calligraphy can be effective.*

In practical terms there is really only one significant difference between combining calligraphy with type and combining calligraphy with calligraphy, or type with type. Calligraphy can produce a far greater visual contrast with type because of its hand-produced cursiveness. When we discussed design it was emphasized that different styles of lettering, whether calligraphy or type, should not be used together if they are very similar in form. Consequently, it is possibly easier to make calligraphy and type work together successfully because of the greater contrast it creates.

When you are working with both calligraphy and type, you will be presented with one of three possible scenarios. Your calligraphy could be larger than the type, the calligraphy and type could be about the same size, or the type could be larger than the calligraphy. For reasons of contrast, as mentioned above, when calligraphy and type are similar in size, you may have to enhance the visual contrast by making the two elements different in colour or tone, even if the letterforms are very different from each other. One or two calligraphic letters in a large size along with small type, especially if the calligraphy has a

WORKING WITH DESIGN

Combining calligraphy and type

you are working with both calligraphy and type you could be presented with one of three possible scenarios. Perhaps your calligraphy could be larger than the type, the calligraphy and type could be about the same size or the type could be larger than the calligraphy. For reasons of contrast mentioned above, when calligraphy and type are similar in size, you may have to enhance the visual contrast by making the two elements different in colour or tone, even if the letterforms are very different from each other. One or two calligraphic letters in a large size along with small type, especially if the calligraphy has a rough-edged effect, can be very dramatic. Using large type with some calligraphy in a small scale has a quite different effect. Avoid using calligraphic typefaces along with your own calligraphy. San serif and roman serifed faces will work much better.

A

A *There is considerable contrast between the larger calligraphy and the small type in this design.*

B *If the calligraphy and type are similar in size it may be necessary to increase the visual contrast by changing colour.*

C *In this layout, making the type much larger than the calligraphy creates the contrast.*

D *A single large calligraphic letter with small type can be effective. Note that the opacity of the large letter has been reduced, showing the texture of the background through the colour, while the type is opaque.*

Seul le silence est grand: tout le reste est faiblesse

Only silence is great: all else is weakness

B

rough-edged effect, can be very dramatic. Using large type with small-scale calligraphy has a quite different effect. Avoid using calligraphic typefaces along with your own calligraphy. Sans-serif and roman-serifed faces will work much better.

One important difference between calligraphy and type in Photoshop is that it is easy to enter large areas of typographic text by simply typing on the keyboard and to edit it using the *Character* and *Paragraph* palettes. From time to time you will encounter the message that your type has to be rasterized (made into a bitmap). For a number of Photoshop processes this has to be done before the operation will work.

The combination of hand lettering and type has been used for many years, long before the advent of computers and Photoshop. It was an expensive option because the lettering designer would have to spend many hours or even days on one or two words for a book cover design or poster. Technically it required the production of a printing block or plate. With Photoshop you can use calligraphy with type for many purposes including such things as invitations, greetings cards, letterheads, and so on. Don't overlook the possibility of using calligraphy and type in your one-off creative pieces. You can modify and manipulate type in exactly the same way as I have described for lettering.

ELEMENTS

C

you are working with both calligraphy and type you could be presented with one of three possible scenarios. Perhaps your calligraphy could be larger than the type, the calligraphy and type could be about the same size or the type could be larger than the calligraphy. For reasons of contrast mentioned above, when calligraphy and type are similar in size, you may have to enhance the visual contrast by making the two elements different in colour or tone, even if the letterforms are very different from each other. One or two calligraphic letters in a large size along with small type, especially if the calligraphy has a rough-edged effect, can be very dramatic. Using large type with some calligraphy in a small scale has a quite different effect. Avoid using calligraphic typefaces along with your own calligraphy. San serif and roman serifed faces will work much better.

Durat, et vosmet rebus servate secundis

D

In some earlier versions of Photoshop, using type was not the most convenient of processes. Even today with Photoshop CS the application is not designed as a typographer's tool. However, with recent versions, inserting, manipulating, and designing with type is as simple as in other bitmap graphics programs.

When you use the *Type* tool in Photoshop, text can be inserted in a document in one of two ways, either as point type or as type within a text frame or bounding box. When you click on your document, a blinking text cursor is inserted. You can then type your text, pressing Return whenever you want a new line to begin. By dragging the *Text* tool over your document, you create a bounding box into which you can type text that wraps onto the next line automatically when it reaches the right-hand edge of the frame. In both cases, the program creates a new text layer. Placing the text cursor over the type lets you edit it. Dragging over it creates a selection. The main text options are displayed in the *Options bar* as well as in the *Character* and *Paragraph* palettes. In addition to the usual options of type size and colour, the *Character* palette lets you adjust the line spacing (leading), letter spacing, and letter width.

WORKING WITH DESIGN

Managing type

120

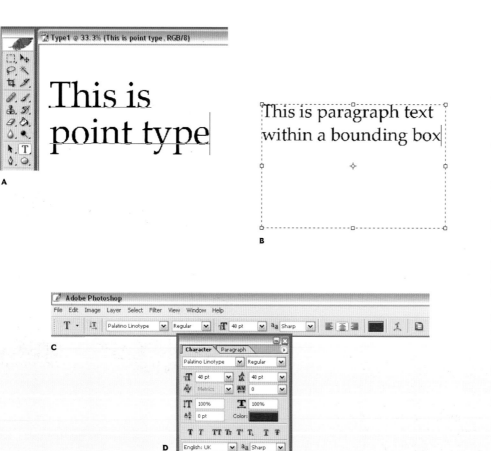

A Click on anywhere in your document with the Text tool to create point type. Using Return starts a new line.

B Dragging the Text tool cursor across the document makes a text frame or bounding box. Text will then wrap automatically from one line to the next.

C The Options bar contains the most common text options.

D The Character palette gives an array of more detailed options.

E Enlarging type won't pixelate the letters unless it is rasterized.

F Make sure you have enough space between lines of text. In this example the lines are much too close together.

G Paragraph text that is aligned with an uneven left-hand margin can be difficult to read.

H A roman typeface, Palatino. Is this more legible than the sans-serif example below?

I This text has been set in Arial, a sans-serif typeface.

When type is created in Photoshop it is vector-based, although not vector-editable without going through the procedures described earlier in the book. This means that you can enlarge text, with the *Transform* command for example, without losing its smooth edge. However, for some procedures the text has to be converted to bitmap by a process called rasterizing. When you request a procedure that requires text to be rasterized, a pop-up will appear and tell you so. Alternatively you can apply the command *Layer>Rasterize>**Type*** at any time.

Design considerations with type are exactly the same as those for calligraphy. Firstly, decide on its purpose. Will someone have to read the text or is it being used as an abstract design? If you want your text to be legible you must give careful consideration to the font, its size, colour,

line spacing, and alignment. Continuous paragraph text in a typeface that has been designed for headlines may be difficult to read. Text that is too small may present problems for people with less than perfect eyesight. If the text colour is too close to that of the background it will not be very visible. If line spacing is too little or too much there will be problems reading continuous text. Similar problems can arise with text that is aligned with a ragged left margin.

Designers may argue whether sans serif or roman typefaces are the more legible, but research has found that in normal reading situations there is no great difference between them. One may be more appropriate than another, perhaps even more legible, in certain cases such as road signs. However, from the calligrapher's perspective, aesthetic considerations will probably be much more important.

Design considerations with type are exactly the same as those for calligraphy. Firstly, decide on its purpose. Will someone have to read the text or is it being used as an abstract design? If you want your text to be legible you must give careful consideration to the font, its, size, colour, line spacing and alignment. **F**

Design considerations with type are exactly the same as those for calligraphy. Firstly, decide on its purpose. Will someone have to read the text or is it being used as an abstract design? If you want your text to be legible you must give careful consideration to the font, its, size, colour, line spacing and alignment. **G**

Design considerations with type are exactly the same as those for calligraphy. Firstly, decide on its purpose. Will someone have to read the text or is it being used as an abstract design? If you want your text to be legible you must give careful consideration to the font, its, size, colour, line spacing and alignment. **H**

Design considerations with type are exactly the same as those for calligraphy. Firstly, decide on its purpose. Will someone have to read the text or is it being used as an abstract design? If you want your text to be legible you must give careful consideration to the font, its, size, colour, line spacing and alignment. **I**

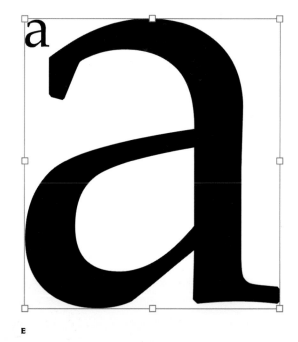

E

In the previous examples we explored the use of single letters from a type font with calligraphy, and calligraphy with continuous typographic text. Photoshop CS adds a new function to its repertoire of type handling options: text can be placed on a path. The orientation of the type can be horizontal or vertical – horizontal type is perpendicular to the path, vertical type is parallel to it. Once the text is put there, it can be edited and modified like any other text, including changing typeface, type size, and colour. The path can be adjusted like any other path and as it changes the text associated with it also changes its path.

PUTTING TEXT ON A PATH

1 To put text on a path, you first need to create a path with the Pen, Line, or Shape tool. Remember that your text will follow the direction in which the path is drawn.

2 Select the Type tool from the Tools Palette and set the text properties to what you want. Click somewhere on the path. This is the insertion point where the text will start from. Type a short piece of text. You will see that it follows the line of the path. Once you have typed some letters or words, try editing them.

3 Using the Shape tool, create an ellipse. Repeat the text entry procedures as in step 2. You will find it easy to create circular text. Try changing the type size.

WORKING WITH DESIGN

More on calligraphy and type

122

As with any use of text that breaks away from the 'normal' horizontal reading line, consideration must be given to legibility factors. As soon as we change the direction of text from the horizontal, we decrease legibility. In some situations this could be important, in others it may not be. Some spectacular visual effects can be created using text following irregular paths, especially when combined with other Photoshop techniques, such as when styles, drop shadows, and fills are applied.

Unfortunately, unless you convert your calligraphy to a font, you cannot put it on a path using this procedure. However, you can use other Photoshop techniques to change straight lines of calligraphy to curves.

The step-by-step examples shown here suggest some possible creative applications of mixing calligraphic shapes with text on a path.

Note – Photoshop's text on a path procedure is very demanding on computer resources. Use it only if you have a fairly powerful computer.

ABCDEFGHIJKL

1

2

3a

3b

5

6

7

CREATING A LETTER WITH TYPE

4 We will now create a letter using nothing but other letters. Firstly, write a letter using a calligraphic brush, ideally using one continuous line.

5 Using the Magnetic Lasso tool create a selection following the line(s) of the letter, keeping the point of the lasso as near to the edges as possible. For certain letters you will have to draw more than one path. Convert the selection to a path.

6 Simplify the path by removing all the unnecessary anchor points, using the Delete Anchor Point tool. Adjust the vectors as necessary. Delete the layer with the initial letter.

7 Select the Type tool and set the typeface to a small size. Click on the path at the point where you want to begin the line. Type some text, or simply some random letters, until you reach the end of the line. Repeat the procedure on any other path.

CREATING A TEXT BORDER

8 This time we will create a text border on a letter and use some colour. Write a letter using a calligraphic brush or import one that you have previously scanned.

9 Using the Magnetic Lasso tool, select the letter. Convert the selection to a vector path using the Make Work Path from Selection option in the Paths palette. More than one path may be created.

10 Change the text colour to one different from the calligraphic letter. Type some text around the path(s). In this example a calligraphic typeface 'Vivaldi' has been used.

11 To make the design more interesting, apply a drop shadow and a style to the background and/or the text.

123

10

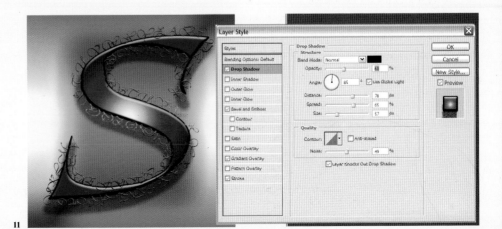

11

If you look through books on calligraphy produced in the last fifty years or so, you will find that a surprisingly small number include illustration. The majority use calligraphy alone. The exceptions to this are presentation documents that include coats of arms, which are, strictly speaking, more akin to design than illustration. Why should this be when we admire the illumination and illustrative decoration in the great manuscripts of the Middle Ages?

There are probably two reasons for this. Firstly, the style of illustration in medieval miniatures is usually rather abstract in its composition, even though the painting is sometimes very realistic. Secondly, the colour pigment and ink that the medieval scribes used had qualities that were sympathetic with each other. Modern pigments don't replicate this quality. Nonfigurative design elements can easily be placed alongside calligraphy. Some styles of illustration work much better with calligraphy than others. Woodcuts or engravings, ideally with limited colour, sit very nicely alongside most calligraphic styles but full colour photographic images do not. Keep the shapes in your designs simple and it will be easier to make them work with your lettering.

WORKING WITH DESIGN

Combining calligraphy and image

O fortunatos nimium, sua si bona norint, Agricolas. Quibus ipsa procul discordibus armis Fundit humo facilem victum Iustissii.

A

O fortunatos nimium, sua si bona norint, Agricolas. Quibus ipsa procul discordibus armis. Fundit humo facilem victum Iustissima tellus.

C

O fortunatos nimium, sua si bona norint, Agricolas. Quibus ipsa procul discordibus armis. Fundit humo facilem victum Iustissima tellus.

B

Although we do not have the secrets of the inks and colours used by scribes of the Middle Ages, we are fortunate today that our technology, in the form of inkjet printers, lets us combine calligraphy, text, and image effectively in a way that was difficult to achieve by hand craftsmanship. Inkjet printing has a distinctive quality, not unlike traditional ink. More importantly, using the same process to print both calligraphy and image produces a level of compatibility. That is not to say that we can't combine processes. There are times where a highly creative solution can be achieved by mixing media: hand-produced calligraphy with printed type, for example.

The layout principles that were explained in the context of calligraphy and type apply equally to text and image. Most images have a structure created by the coincidence of critical points and lines. Look for the structure in illustrations and use it to determine the best place for the text. Be careful with text overlaid on an image and consider the effect each has on the other. It is technically easy now to use such effects as 'reversing out', where lettering is white on a black or coloured illustration background. If you find it difficult to design calligraphy with illustration, try using the space around them to help hold the design together. Margins and spaces between design elements are as much part of the design as the calligraphy and illustration.

If you plan to sell your work, you must be very careful about copyright and ensure that the illustration that you are using is no longer protected or that you have permission to use it.

O fortunatos nimium, sua
si bona norint, Agricolas.
Quibus ipsa procul discordibus
armis. Fundit humo faciem
victum lustissima tellus.

A *Simple images such as woodcuts work well with calligraphy. Simple lines and flat colour coordinate well with the script lettering.*

B *No matter how carefully a photographic image is placed alongside calligraphy it rarely produces a satisfactory result. When both text and photograph are printed on an inkjet printer the process helps to bring them together visually.*

C *One way to make photographs and other real-world images work with calligraphy is to make them very small. The image then becomes almost like an icon.*

D *Most images can be analyzed using lines that aid in identifying the structure within them. These lines can help to determine the position of text and illustration.*

E *Even photographs have structure that can help to determine the layout. Using a single colour and reducing the tone of the image, as in this example, can help to coordinate calligraphy and photographs.*

D

O fortunatos nimium, sua
si bona norint, Agricolas.
Quibus ipsa procul discordibus
armis. Fundit humo faciem
victum lustissima tellus.

E

The following step-by-step exercises demonstrate the two different approaches to design, the first using a grid identified in the illustration to help position the other elements, the second where all of the parts that make up the whole design are arranged visually until they 'look right'. The former method usually, but not always, produces a rather formal effect that is appropriate for certain applications. Even if a design is formal, it doesn't have to be less creative in its concept.

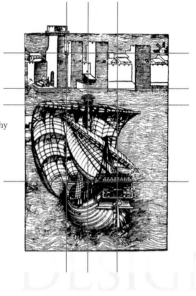

2

Spain

from Gordon's Geography

1725

1

Step-by-step example 1

126

Spain, formerly Iberia, Hisperia, by some Spania, and now bounded on the East by part of the Mediterranian Sea, on the West by Portugal and part of the vast Atlantic Ocean, on the North by the Bay of Biscay; and the South by the Straights of Gibralter, is termed by the Italians, Spagna, by its natives Espana, by the French Espagne, by the Germans Spanien, and by the English Spain, so called (as some say) from a certain King nam'd Hispanus, other from the Greek Spania (veritas vel penuria) becaue of its scarcity of inhabitants. But the most received opinion is that it came from Hispalis (now Seville) the chief city of the whole country in former times.

3

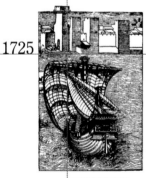

1725

Spain, formerly Iberia, Hisperia, by some Spania, and now bounded on the East by part of the Mediterranian Sea, on the West by Portugal and part of the vast Atlantic Ocean, on the North by the Bay of Biscay; and the South by the Straights of Gibralter, is termed by the Italians, Spagna, by its natives Espana, by the French Espagne, by the Germans Spanien, and by the English Spain, so called (as some say) from a certain King nam'd Hispanus, other from the Greek Spania (veritas vel penuria) becaue of its scarcity of inhabitants. But the most received opinion is that it came from Hispalis (now Seville) the chief city of the whole country in former times.

from Gordon's Geography

4

1 *Start a new document. Find an illustration that you would like to use for the exercise. Choose something other than a photograph. If it is not already a digital image, scan it and import it into your document. The size of the image in relation to your canvas or page doesn't matter at this stage. Find some text that relates in some way to the image. Include a heading and one or two other pieces of text, such as a caption for the illustration. In the example, we have the main text, a heading ('Spain'), a subheading ('from Gordon's Geography'), and a date ('1725'). Type the text in a typeface of your choice so that each text element is on a different layer. Give the file a name and save it. We will use this document as a temporary store for the illustration and text. We could have used this document for the final piece but the principles will be clearer if we work this way.*

2 *Examine your illustration carefully and draw straight horizontal and vertical lines where you can identify structure as explained previously.*

3 *Begin a new document but keep the first one on screen. Cut and paste the illustration (without the structure lines) and the text into the new document, keeping each element on a separate layer. Starting with the main text, position it somewhere on your page so that the top, bottom, or left margin aligns with one of the structure lines that you identified. Refer back to your other document if necessary. Change the typeface, type size, line spacing, or column width if you wish.*

1725 *Spain*

Spain, formerly Iberia, Hisperia, by some Spania, and now bounded on the East by part of the Mediterranean Sea, on the West by Portugal and part of the vast Atlantic Ocean, on the North by the Bay of Biscay; and the South by the Straights of Gibraltar, is termed by the Italians, Spagna, by its natives Espana, by the French Espagne, by the Germans Spanien, and by the English Spain, so called (as some say) from a certain King nam'd Hispanus, other from the Greek Spania (veritas vel penuria) becaue of its scarcity of inhabitants. But the most received opinion is that it came from Hispalis (now Seville) the chief city of the whole country in former times.

from Gordon's Geography

5

1725 *pain*

Spain, formerly Iberia, Hisperia, by some Spania, and now bounded on the East by part of the Mediterranean Sea, on the West by Portugal and part of the vast Atlantic Ocean, on the North by the Bay of Biscay; and the South by the Straights of Gibraltar, is termed by the Italians, Spagna, by its natives Espana, by the French Espagne, by the Germans Spanien, and by the English Spain, so called (as some say) from a certain King nam'd Hispanus, other from the Greek Spania (veritas vel penuria) becaue of its scarcity of inhabitants. But the most received opinion is that it came from Hispalis (now Seville) the chief city of the whole country in former times.

from Gordon's Geography

6

1725 *pain*

Spain, formerly Iberia, Hisperia, by some Spania, and now bounded on the East by part of the Mediterranean Sea, on the West by Portugal and part of the vast Atlantic Ocean, on the North by the Bay of Biscay; and the South by the Straights of Gibraltar, is termed by the Italians, Spagna, by its natives Espana, by the French Espagne, by the Germans Spanien, and by the English Spain, so called (as some say) from a certain King nam'd Hispanus, other from the Greek Spania (veritas vel penuria) becaue of its scarcity of inhabitants. But the most received opinion is that it came from Hispalis (now Seville) the chief city of the whole country in former times.

from Gordon's Geography

7

4 Now locate the text elements other than the heading. Don't place them in the most obvious positions but relate them in some way to the structure lines of the illustration.

*5 Write the heading in a calligraphic style that you think is appropriate for the subject. In the example a fairly formal italic has been used. Adjust the size and, if you wish, the proportion (*Image>Transform>**Scale**)*. Drag the heading to a position that corresponds with one of the image structure lines.*

6 Everything now looks as if it has been designed. Each element appears to be in the right place – but the design is not very interesting and we haven't used colour. Remove the first letter of your heading and rewrite it on a separate layer. Scale this initial letter so that it is slightly larger than the illustration, and locate it over it. You may have to change the order of layers in the Layers *palette. Reduce the* Opacity *to 50%.*

7 Let's add a bit of colour and some interest to the heading. Choose or create a filter and apply it to the heading, but not the initial letter. Adjust the colour of the initial letter so that it coordinates with the rest of the heading. Now apply a filter if you wish. Finally, crop your design to its finished size.

This example takes you through the process of designing with image and text in a free, visual way, adjusting each element as necessary until everything appears to be in the right position, scale, and colour. Although this is a step-by-step exercise, in reality the procedure is very much that of trial and error. If one part of a layout or design doesn't work, simply step backward and try something else. It is a good idea to try out your ideas on others. Their tastes and sensitivity to colour and scale may not be the same as yours.

Step-by-step example 2

1 Start a new document. We will use a few calligraphic letters, some type, and an image. This will avoid having to relate the specific text to the image and focus attention on the visual design process. Write three or four calligraphic letters in black using a calligraphic brush. Type five or six letters in different typefaces and in different colours. Choose colours that work well together, although these can be changed afterward. Find an image (not photographic) that you can use in the project. Make sure that each element, that is each individual letter and the image, is on a separate layer.

2 Create or apply a different filter to each of the calligraphic letters. Try to coordinate the colours with those that you chose for the typeface letters. In the example, a default Glass Button from the Styles palette has been applied to two of the letters and a gradient fill to the third.

3 As with the previous exercise we will use one document as a store for the design elements. Open a second document. Cut and paste one of the calligraphic letters and the image into your new page. Begin working on your design. In the illustration, the 'B' can be placed over the image as the upper part of the gradient fill is lighter than the leaves of the plant. Adjust the scale of both the image and the letter. It is best if they are not too similar in size.

4 *Cut and paste the other two calligraphic letters. Drag the other two calligraphic letters into a position that looks right, scaling them as necessary. When you position elements of a design so that they overlap, be careful that you don't create any new awkward or undesirable shapes. This is particularly important with letters.*

5 *Now cut and paste one of the typographic letters and position it where it looks well in relation to the first part of the design.*

6 *Position the rest of the typographic letters.*

7 *At this point you may wish to readjust the size and position of some of the design elements. In the illustration the calligraphic 'C' has been repositioned.*

8 *Add a suitable background and crop the canvas to complete the design. Create several designs with the same elements, building up the composition in a different order each time. When you examine your design carefully, you may find that you have subconsciously created and worked with structural lines. If you have done this, it indicates that your design sense is developing well!*

A *Three pages from the author's website showing a gallery of calligraphic work.*

B *Computer-aided calligraphy by the author, shot-blasted on sandstone. The lettering was supplied to the monumental mason as a computer file. The design was then transferred using computer-controlled cutters.*

OUTPUT
Output forms

130

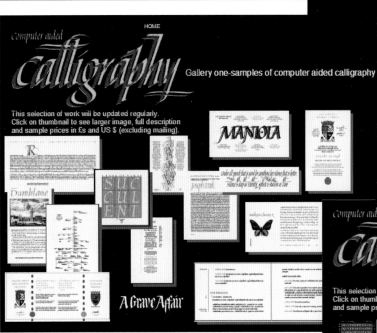

The final outcome of traditional calligraphy written with ink or another colour medium on paper is usually a single piece of artwork that is an end in itself. This could be for framing, as a presentation document, a manuscript book, or similar application. If traditional calligraphy is produced as artwork to be used in commercial printing, perhaps for a book cover or poster, or as the basis for a script typeface design, it is usually modified in some way to suit the process. Hand-rendered calligraphy is sometimes used on other materials such as glass and stone.

With the use of computer graphics applications, including Photoshop, the range of methods by which calligraphy can be created, modified, and used is extended considerably. Handwritten lettering can be scanned and imported into a document or it can be created digitally on screen. The process of correcting, retouching, and creating effects has been made very much easier, as we have seen throughout the book. The range of output forms and the methods by which these can be handled by an array of other computer-controlled equipment is extensive. Not least, the variety of methods by which calligraphy can be displayed and turned into some tangible form, such as print, at a very modest cost is beginning to change the way that some calligraphers work.

Very few calligraphers see the final version of their work as virtual, that is to be seen only as a digital image on a computer screen. Perhaps this is, in part, because we still consider real calligraphic artworks to be on paper or some other physical surface. Certainly, as we shall see, computer calligraphy printed by inkjet on carefully chosen papers has a unique quality quite different from the computer display version. However, it is now so easy to design webpages that it is perfectly practical to exhibit your calligraphic masterpieces to the world via the Internet.

Another way calligraphy produced using Photoshop can be used is as artwork for use in other applications, especially page makeup software such as InDesign or QuarkXPress. Export to other applications is now much easier than it used to be. With the more recent versions of the Windows and Macintosh operating systems, often an image can simply be dragged from one program to another or, at most, cut from one application and pasted into the other. Previously, an image had to be saved in a file format the other application could read. Calligraphic ideas worked out in Photoshop and other graphics programs can be used as the basis for typeface designs, in which case they have to be transferred to a program such as Fontographer.

As we will see, the subtleties of colour integrity that are so important in a photographic image, especially one that includes skin tones, are not nearly as critical in calligraphic work. For example, it is unlikely that reducing the number of colours in a piece of digital calligraphy from millions to 256 would have any significant effect on the design. Considerations of such issues as resolution and image size are far more important in retaining the quality of the image.

B

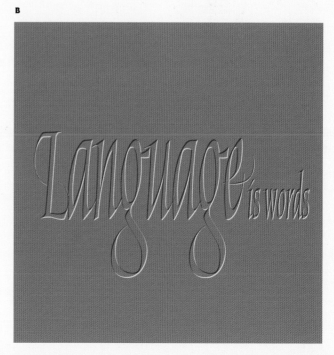

A laser printer is a useful piece of equipment for calligraphic work in black and white on a small scale. It has the advantage that double-sided prints can be made without one side showing through to the other – the scourge of inkjet printers, except when they are used with the thickest papers. The quality of print, in terms of both resolution and colour, is now such that an inkjet is currently the best printer on which to produce hard copy of your calligraphy. Size will always be a restricting factor and it is unlikely that an individual will own an inkjet printer that can print large sheet sizes. Some inkjets can be 'tweaked' to print slightly larger sizes than that quoted for the machine, especially if they can use continuous paper, in which case, if you are lucky, the height or width of the document (but not both) is restricted only by the availability of paper.

When you are printing your calligraphy there are no issues that need any special consideration, at least not compared with the way that you will usually work when you are printing images. There are, however, some aspects of the process of which you should be aware or that may be used to your advantage.

OUTPUT

Printing

A Complex calligraphy on a coloured background.

B A simple frame around your calligraphy can sometimes enhance it. This pale yellow frame has been added directly in Photoshop.

C Inkjet print on an absorbent paper. Note how the ink tends to follow the texture of the paper. This effect could sometimes be desirable but not if you want a good, crisp edge to your lettering.

D If paper is not stored in dry conditions, inkjet print can smudge.

The ink used in inkjet printers is translucent. Consequently, it is impossible to get a solid black or colour. If you print on white paper, the effect of the ink's translucency is to produce a slightly lighter tone. The colour will retain its brilliance and may even be enhanced by the white surface. If you print on a coloured paper, its colour will affect the colour of the ink. The extent to which this happens depends on the richness of the paper colour. Some papers are highly absorbent and the ink can spread, making the paper useless for this purpose. Even less absorbent papers that have been stored in slightly damp conditions can react in the same way. Heavily coated papers also encourage ink to spread across the surface and these too should be avoided. Paper types will be considered in more detail in the next section. Most inkjet printer manufacturers tell you not to use cut paper or paper with a torn edge. The heads of the printer travel back and forth very close to the paper surface. If they encounter any parts raised, the ink will smudge or, even worse, the paper will jam.

A complex piece of calligraphy may benefit from being framed. It may also be helped if it is placed within a mount of a suitable colour. In Photoshop you can create a frame around your work that may enhance it whether or not it will be put in a frame afterward. With your document open, choose *Image>***Canvas Size**. Enter the new size of your canvas, making sure that *Relative* is not selected. Alternatively, you can select *Relative* and enter the amount by which you want to increase your canvas width and height. Select a foreground colour for the frame and use the *Paint Bucket* tool to fill it.

C

D

E

E *The* Canvas Size *dialog box can be reached through the* Image *menu. The* Anchor *setting controls where the extra canvas will be added. Leaving it in the middle means that the extra canvas will be distributed equally around the existing canvas, setting the original canvas to the left means that all of the extra will be added to the right of it, and so on.*

Using high-quality paper gives a touch of class to your calligraphy. It is also likely that your work will be more permanent and the colours less likely to fade if you choose your paper carefully. The papers that may be considered to be useful fall into three categories, namely white, coloured, and special.

The choice of white paper depends largely on the purpose of your lettering. Is it an ephemeral piece that you, or someone else, will throw away after a short time? Is it more important but doesn't have to have a life of many years? Or is it a masterpiece that you hope will not turn yellow and will retain its colours for decades or even hundreds of years? If you want your work to last, choose paper that is acid free. The low pH chemicals in some papers quickly turn them yellow. Poor-quality paper, even if acid free, may have intrusions that will eventually cause foxing, the unsightly yellow-brown marks that we often find on old books. Good acid-free papers are made mostly for the artists' market and are usually mould-made. They can be purchased in good artists' materials shops. However, they are rather expensive and are very prone to crushing. Check every sheet that you buy since even a slight

OUTPUT

Papers

B

A

C

D

kink can spoil your work. The majority of mould-made papers are rather rough to be used in an inkjet printer for calligraphy. Having said that, the great thing about inkjet printing is that you can print calligraphy on surfaces that would be impossible to write on by traditional methods. The rough mould-made papers are called 'knot'. However, most manufacturers produce paper with a 'hot pressed' surface that is smooth and ideal for inkjet printing.

Coloured papers, even the better ones such as Ingres, are problematic if permanence is important. Reds are especially prone to fading and prints must be protected from long exposure to sunlight. A much better solution to coloured paper is to print your own coloured background. This will stand the test of time. Use special coloured papers only if you have to and if they will be stored in the dark.

You can consider any other type of paper as 'special'. Even some inexpensive throwaway materials such as brown wrapping paper can be used. There are many beautiful papers from Thailand, Japan, or China. Many of these have intrusions of leaves and other organic material. The very strong markings on some of these papers will not go well with your lettering. There are many that are much more subtle and can be used to great effect. Some Thai and Japanese papers are too thin to run through an inkjet printer. Taping the paper lightly to a thicker sheet of paper and feeding both through the printer can solve this. The bleedthrough effect on the supporting paper can sometimes be as visually interesting as the original calligraphy! Some inkjet printers will even handle thin cloth taped to a paper background in this way.

E

F

A *The rough or deckle edge on hand- and mould-made papers can be left untrimmed for effect.*

B *Red dye in coloured paper will fade very quickly when exposed to light. It is much better to colour and print your own background.*

C *The texture of some papers can be a little too dominant for calligraphy. This one is just about acceptable.*

D *Not all papers have strong textures. Some are fairly subtle.*

E *This Thai paper is beautiful but may be a bit dark for inkjet printing, even in black.*

F *Even brown wrapping paper can be used to print calligraphy on an inkjet printer.*

Calligraphy can be handwritten, reproduced by mechanical printing processes, cut into a wood block, carved in stone, engraved on glass, or, as we have been examining in this book, created and manipulated in the computer and output to a range of printers or displays. Every different output method imparts its own characteristics to the lettering. So lettering printed on a laser printer will look different from that printed on an inkjet and different again from the same lettering written with pen and ink. Even the display on a computer monitor will be only an approximation of the final work on paper.

The output from a monochrome high-resolution laser printer superficially resembles commercial lithographic printing. The black is solid and the edges of the letters are crisp and smooth, unless examined through a strong magnifier. Inkjet printing, as we have seen, has a unique translucency. Traditional calligraphy written with ink or artists' watercolour on paper can range from solid to very translucent and the smoothness of the edges of the lettering depends a great deal on the texture of the paper surface. We can make use of these different qualities to create interest and variety in calligraphy. For example, a

OUTPUT

Combining processes

ex libris

A

C

ex libris

B

A Handwritten calligraphy with ink is affected by the texture of the paper.

B Computer calligraphy printed on an inkjet printer is translucent and lets other colours shine through.

C Overprinting the same or different images several times on an inkjet printer can produce some interesting effects.

page of laser-printed text can be overprinted in colour with calligraphy on an inkjet printer or inkjet-printed calligraphy could then have some handwritten text added afterward. Multiple scans of handwritten lettering can be worked on in Photoshop for display on screen or output to print. Overprinting several times on an inkjet printer can produce some very interesting effects.

You should be aware of some technical considerations. Several processes are unadvisable and could damage your equipment. Never run paper with watercolour or gouache on it through a laser printer. These media contain gums or other binding materials that can be deposited on the printer drum, causing permanent damage. Black ink can also flake off but is not usually so problematic. Some inkjet inks can also react badly because of the heat

generated in a laser printer, although this is usually restricted to fading. Most inkjet inks can dissolve non-waterproof ink and watercolour paint. There are now waterproof inkjet inks on the market so, if you are planning to mix handwritten lettering with waterproof inkjet print, it would be best to print this first.

Once you start producing calligraphy with Photoshop you will soon be frustrated by the restrictive maximum size your printer can handle. One way around this is the use of collage or montage. You could consider designs made of different parts that combine into a single piece of work. With some careful planning and creative thinking, it is possible to produce calligraphy on a large scale. Ensure that your craftsmanship is of a high quality – cut paper very carefully and accurately, and use adhesives with care.

D *Computer calligraphy printed on a laser printer is solid and retains the smooth edges of the lettering.*

E *One solution to the size restrictions of printers is to design the calligraphy in parts. This design is composed of five different sections joined together. The vertical paper weaving hides the joins.*

ex libris

D

E

The great advances in recent years in making computer software more user-friendly has been of particular value to those who work with several different programs simultaneously and regularly transfer files of various sorts from one application or operating system to another. The earliest integrated programs enabled users to take a file from one module to another as if it were part of the same software – which it really was. But there were problems of compatibility, especially when it came to transferring image files from one program to another. There was only a limited range of common file formats that could be read by most programs and some of these, such as JPEG and GIF, were designed specifically to make file transfer easier.

How things have changed. Not only can most graphics software read many common file formats, but there is also relatively easy transfer between PC and Macintosh platforms. Even the method of moving a file to another program is a simple drag and drop procedure in an increasing number of applications and the chances are that both text and image can be simply cut and then pasted into another program from the clipboard.

OUTPUT

Exporting to other applications

There can still be compatibility problems if you choose certain option settings with some file formats. Even with the widely used TIFF format you can sometimes encounter a program that won't read it if it has been saved with a specific setting. For example, a few programs will not recognize TIFFs that are saved with LZW compression.

If drag and drop doesn't work, the next option is cut and paste. If file transfer is the preferred procedure, then Photoshop offers 16 format options. This is fewer than most computer graphics applications, especially when six of these are Photoshop's own formats. However, you will not find this a limitation. Photoshop is also eccentric in using the *File>***Save As** command to include what other programs would call 'export'. The only specific export command is one that may be handy if you use Illustrator and is executed through *File>Export>***Paths to Illustrator**. Photoshop layers may not be recognized by some programs and, obviously, will not be available in applications that do not work in that way. Another problem you may encounter is with software versions. Few of us can afford to keep up to date with the most recent version of all the software on our computers. The charges that some software companies make for their upgrades are frequently prohibitive. This can mean that if you save a file in an up-to-date program's raw format and try to import it into an early version of another program it is highly likely that it will not be possible. In the case of text this is easily solved with the use of Rich Text Format (RTF). Unfortunately, there is no simple solution to this in the case of graphics files, although usually you can save in a standard format such as TIFF, JPEG, or BMP.

A *Different file formats can be reached from the* Save As *menu.*

B *JPG (JPEG): Joint Photographic Experts Group.*

C *TIF (TIFF): Tagged Image File Format.*

D *BMP: Windows bitmap.*

E *GIF: Graphic Interchange Format.*

F *PNG: Portable Network Graphic.*

G *TGA: Truevision Targa.*

H *PCX: Zsoft PC Paintbrush.*

I *PCT (PICT): Macintosh image.*

Photoshop is bundled with a companion program called ImageReady that can be used to edit and create Web graphics. The design of webpages and the detailed preparation of images for Web display are beyond the scope of this book. However, here we examine the issues that relate to calligraphic images and how these can be best displayed in a Web browser. The main considerations are how to achieve a balance between file sizes and image quality. The choice of methodology for the display of calligraphy on the Web is not necessarily the same as that for the display of photographic images.

Although calligraphy can use the same spectrum of colours as any other imagery, a reduction to an 8-bit/256-colour Web-safe palette is not usually a problem. Retaining the sharpness of the calligraphy is far more important. Files on the Web are compressed to reduce their size. In practice this comes down to a choice of JPEG or GIF formats. The other common format is PNG, but some older browsers don't support it. JPEG supports millions of colours while GIF supports only 256. Which format you use depends on whether your calligraphy includes such things as gradients that perhaps require a greater colour range.

OUTPUT

Displaying calligraphy on the World Wide We

Original: "Web1.tif"
22M

GIF
251.7K
90 sec @ 28.8 Kbps
100% dither
Selective palette
256 colors

GIF
227.3K
82 sec @ 28.8 Kbps
100% dither
Selective palette
128 colors

JPEG
319.1K
114 sec @ 28.8 Kbps
100 quality

3b

GIF
251.7K
90 sec @ 28.8 Kbps

GIF
227.3K
82 sec @ 28.8 Kbps
100% dither
Selective palette
128 colors

JPEG
319.1K
114 sec @ 28.8 Kbps

3c

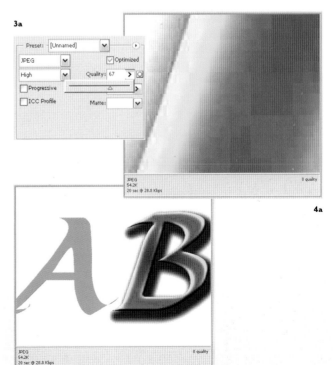

3a

Preset: [Unnamed]
JPEG
High — Quality: 67 — Optimized
Progressive
ICC Profile — Matte:

JPEG
54.2K
20 sec @ 28.8 Kbps
0 quality

4a

JPEG
54.2K
20 sec @ 28.8 Kbps
0 quality

4b

1 *Start a new document with the colour depth setting at 16 bits. Write two calligraphic letters. Leave one in a solid colour and apply a filter with a range of colours and tones to the other.*

2 *Apply the command* File>**Save for Web**. *Photoshop generates three optimization settings and also shows the original image. It even displays the time in seconds that it would take to download the image. Note the effect of each method. The 100% dither with a 128-colour palette (lower left) is grainy while the 0% dither with 256 colours has broken the graduations into discrete colour bands, although these are only noticeable when the image is enlarged. Either method may be suitable in this instance, depending on the importance of the reduced file size. In some* situations, the 0% dither with 256 colours may be better for flat colour work, as there is only a slight loss of colour depth in the first letter.

3 *Select JPEG in the Presets pop-up menu. In our example the default maximum quality setting has reduced the original file size from 22 megabytes to a little over 311 kilobytes. There is little evidence of quality loss, even on enlargement.*

4 *In the Presets pop-up menu change the Quality to 0 either by dragging the slider or by typing the numeric value. The quality has now greatly deteriorated but the file size has been reduced to only 54.2 kilobytes. However, even when the image is compressed by this amount, the quality loss is not noticeable at the reduced scale.*

It is probable that the calligraphy you produce will be printed on your own printer or, perhaps, by a bureau. Photoshop provides the facility to process colour images for commercial printing, including the preparation of colour separations. If your calligraphy is to be used in a commercial situation, such as a poster, or if it is to be reproduced in a book, it is unlikely that you will become involved in the technical aspects of print reproduction by lithographic or other means. However, some unexpected things can happen to your work if you are not aware of the changes that can take place when your image is processed and sent to press.

If your calligraphy is solid black and white, it can be very accurately printed. If it is monochrome (black, greys, and white), printing will affect only the smoothness of the edges of letters, because the image will be converted into a pattern of very small dots. Very early on in this book we explored the various colour modes and found that the three RGB channels of red, green, and blue could render a spectrum of millions of colours on a computer screen. As commercial print processes usually use only four colours, cyan, magenta, yellow, and black, changes are inevitable in the final appearance of your work. If you have worked on

OUTPUT

Supplying artwork for commercial printing

A

B

your calligraphy in RGB mode you can, very simply, change to CMYK mode by using *Image>**Mode***. This will let you see whether there will be any significant changes to colour when it passes through the print process. You don't have to supply your file in CMYK mode. Every print store will be familiar with Photoshop and standard file formats and can make any conversions necessary for their operational methods.

You could find yourself in the situation where you would like a very special solid colour for a part of your work, or even a varnish, and it could be undesirable or impossible to have this printed by the usual four-colour process. An example may be a decorative large initial letter. In such cases a spot colour, necessitating an additional printing plate, can be used. There are cost implications, of course. A spot colour is added to an image by creating a spot-colour channel. In the *Channels* palette choose *New Spot Channel*. In the dialog box that will be displayed, select *Custom* in the *Color Picker*. This will display the PANTONE colour range, which accurately matches printing inks, from which you can select a spot colour that will be reproduced accurately in the final print. When you click *OK*, a spot-colour channel with the PANTONE name will be added to the *Channels* palette. The spot colour is printed last and will overlie the other four colours. Printing inks are not opaque, so the image below will shine through. Unless you want this effect, which to some extent defeats the purpose of using the additional colour, use spot colour only when it is on a clear, white background.

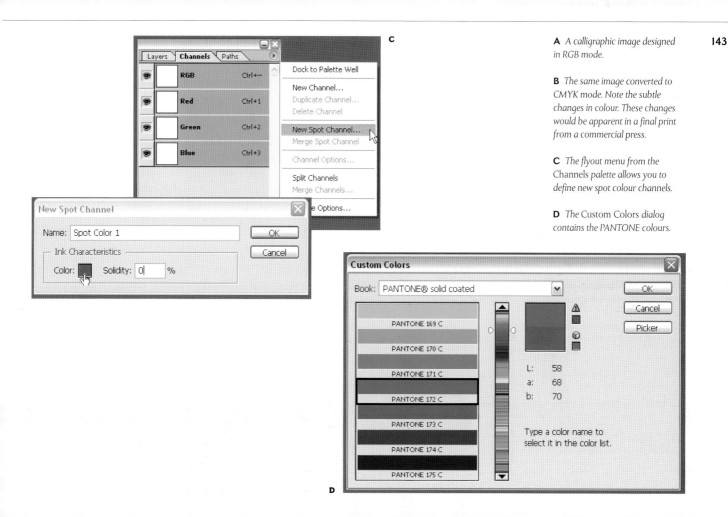

A *A calligraphic image designed in RGB mode.*

B *The same image converted to CMYK mode. Note the subtle changes in colour. These changes would be apparent in a final print from a commercial press.*

C *The flyout menu from the* Channels *palette allows you to define new spot colour channels.*

D *The* Custom Colors *dialog contains the PANTONE colours.*

The following projects are designed to illustrate the use of calligraphy with Photoshop for a number of very different situations, ranging from a commercial application to what is, in effect, fine art. They also demonstrate the combined use of many of the techniques and processes that have been described throughout the book. Although the step-by-step instructions are specific to each of the example topics and are based on the actual words used, you are encouraged to adapt each element of the procedures to an application and word or words of your choice. In these projects the instructions are not as detailed as those given previously throughout the book. Where appropriate, reference is given to the page in the book where the method used is described in more detail so that you can recap on anything with which you are not fully familiar.

SOME WORKED EXAMPLES

Introduction

144

DESIGNING A LOGO

The term 'logo' is a corruption of 'logotype', which was originally used to describe a distinctive cipher or symbol of a company, organization or other establishment based on lettering. Now the term is used to apply to any company symbol or trademark. In this project, calligraphic lettering is created and modified to make a 'word shape' that could be used as a logo. It involves the use of vectors in Photoshop. Vallum means the rampart of an ancient Roman fort.

1 *Start a new document with a white background. Ensure that the resolution is at least 300 pixels/inch. Choose a word that you want to use as the basis of your design. Write the word freely in black using a calligraphic brush in Photoshop. Alternatively, write it with a pen on paper, scan it, and import it into Photoshop (see pages 46–47).*

2 *Examine the lettering and try to identify aspects that could be used to make the design distinctive. In our example we can retain or even emphasize the way the vertical of the 'a' drops below the writing line and make use of the informal diagonal end to some of the letters. However, there are also elements that are less desirable, including poor letter spacing and the way the letters are out of line.*

1

2

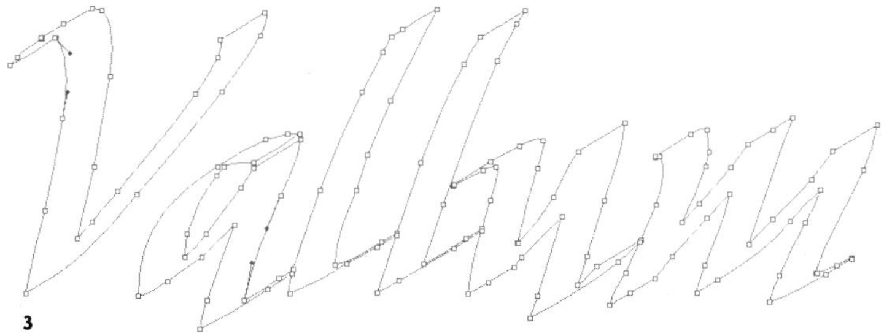

3

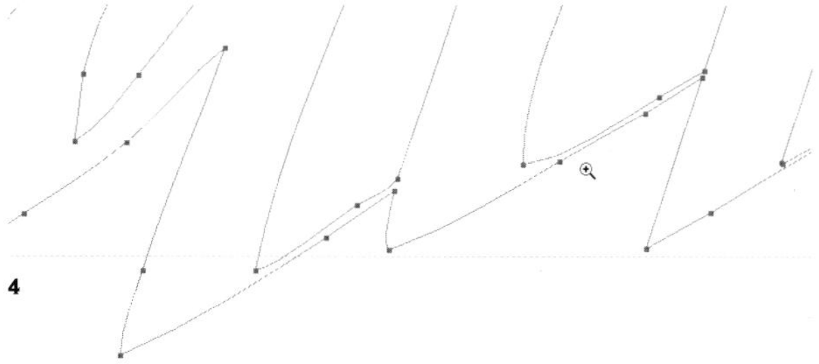

4

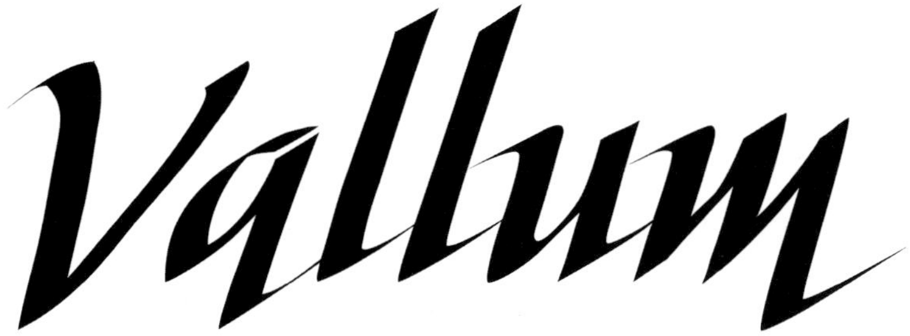

5-6

7

8

3 *Select the lettering using the* Magic Wand *tool and convert the selection to a path by using* Make Work Path from Selection *in the* Paths *palette. Delete the layer with the solid letter to reveal the vector outlines (see pages 70–71).*

4 *You may find it helpful now to drag guidelines from the rulers for the top and bottom of the x-height. In our example the vector paths, other than that of the initial capital, are continuous. If you have to separate letters, you can delete segments by selecting them and pressing Backspace. Delete unnecessary anchor points but be careful not to distort the letterforms. Drag groups of anchor points to line up the lettering as necessary. Adjust the letter spacing. The Undo option will very useful at this stage. Repeatedly using the* Fill Path with Foreground Color *option then stepping backward will let you see the consequence of making changes to the paths.*

5 *Adjust the part of the 'a' that drops below the line and echo this in the 'm'.*

6 *A great deal of adjustment is needed to the lettering to improve the letterform but to retain the informality as much as possible. When all these adjustments have been made, examine the design.*

7 *The design still lacks a distinctive character. Add a flourish to the initial letter 'V' (see pages 74–75).*

8 *The design is completed by adding a style filter effect.*

Formal penmanship is still the foundation on which professional calligraphers base their work. However, contemporary calligraphy places much more emphasis on expressive creativity than has been the case in the past. The interaction between the creative mind, the skilled hand, the writing instrument, and the writing surface is now seen to be of great value. Western scribes are now exploring the abstract qualities that are so much part of Chinese, Japanese, and, to a lesser extent, Arabic calligraphy. While there are not the spiritual overtones evident in the East, the notion that calligraphy can be an outpouring of the soul is being grasped in Britain, Europe, Australia, and the USA. This example uses calligraphic forms that are based on language but are not necessarily legible script.

Photoshop is great for the creation of spontaneous forms based on line and shape. Indeed, it is far more suited to this than to any formal application. The only satisfactory way to use the *Calligraphic Brush* tool, for instance, is to write very quickly so that the lines flow smoothly and without evidence of hesitation. It takes practice, but costs nothing but time to try the same calligraphic form repeatedly, stepping back until the desired outcome is achieved.

SOME WORKED EXAMPLES

Calligraphic form

146

1 *Using a calligraphic brush on separate documents, write some 'words' in black on white but concentrate on the calligraphic lines that you are making, rather than on legibility or on keeping the letters straight and equal in size. Write quickly and spontaneously. Try to use smooth, continuous strokes. Write the same word over and over again until you are close to something with which you are satisfied. Adjust or correct the form if you wish using the vector graphics options in Photoshop. Save each of the versions that you want to keep in different files. Open a new document and paste the first of your calligraphic forms into it. Using the* Magic Wand *tool make a copy of the form and paste it into a new layer.*

2 Apply a Gaussian Blur to the original layer.

3 Colour the copied layer with any colour other than that of the original. Using a crisp overlay on a blurred layer is a simple way of creating an effect on the most basic of calligraphic shapes.

4 Try changing the colour of the calligraphic form to which you applied the Gaussian Blur on each of the other forms that you wrote and saved.

5 The shaded colour effect can be enhanced by adding an Outer Glow of a slightly different colour.

6 Using some of the other filters and styles can be dramatic but verges on cliché, as in the case of the Pillow Emboss filter. Some do produce desirable effects when used with restraint, such as the Plaster filter.

7 This final version is more complex than it looks. It comprises five layers each with a different fill or filter applied. The first is coloured in addition to a Gaussian Blur, then a Chrome filter, a Paint Daubs filter, another Gaussian Blur, and a colour filled background. The order of the layers was adjusted to achieve the best effect.

2

3

4

5a

5b

6b

6a

6c

7

This example is a paperless exercise, creating desktop computer wallpaper. In more complex calligraphic applications you may have to use a large number of layers. Although this can often be avoided, it is worthwhile gaining experience of multilayer work. In the example shown here the number of layers is limited, but you are encouraged to go well beyond this and add more and more layers to produce a richly textured design. The alphabet has been used as the basis of the design together with an initial letter. The text can be anything that you consider to be appropriate and the initial letter can be any.

1a

1b

A calligraphic desktop

1 Open a new document. Make sure that you set up the page to the same aspect ratio as your monitor. The best way to do this is to work on exactly the same pixel-by-pixel dimensions as the display with which you work. Choose a dark background colour and select this via the dialog box (if you have already set it in the Toolbox) or fill the blank canvas with the Paint Bucket tool. Write the letters of the alphabet (or some other appropriate wording). You can do this directly on a new layer in your document or, better still, write it in a separate document, copy it then paste it into the new layer. If you prefer, you can scan some calligraphy that you have written on paper and import it. Colour the lettering and rescale it as necessary.

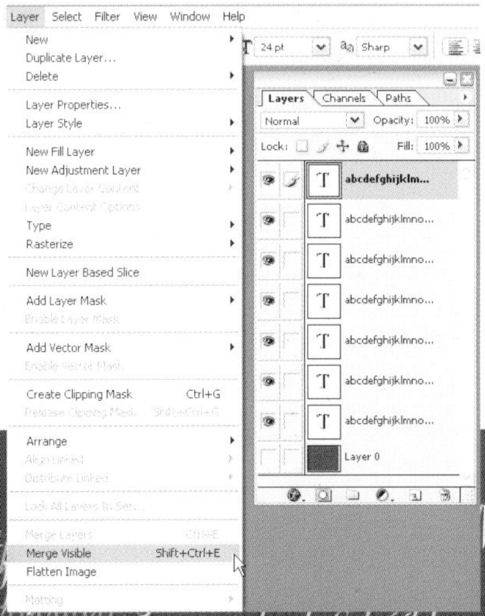

3

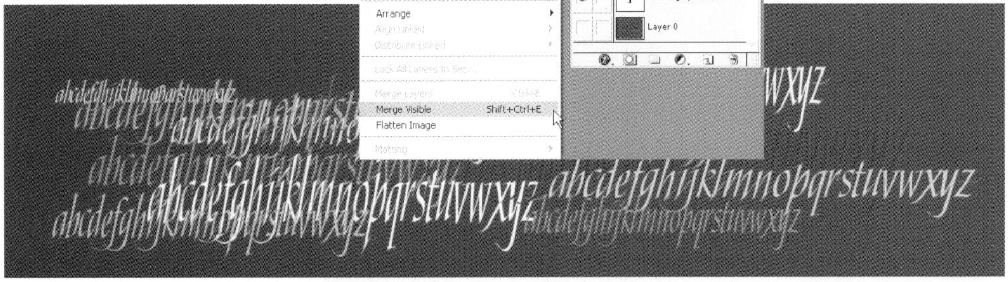

2

4

2 *With a copy of the lettering on the clipboard, paste the lettering repeatedly into new layers, changing the colour and the size each time. Try to build up a well-balanced design. You will require some space for desktop icons so leave an area either at the side, above or below.*

3 *When you are happy with the design, merge the lettering together but not with the background. The easiest way to do this is to make only the lettering layers visible and apply the command* Layers>**Merge Visible**. *The lettered design then becomes a single layer that can be moved as a group (see pages 114–115).*

4 *Using the Magic Wand tool with the composite lettering layer active, select the area around the lettering. Select several areas within the lettering also, but not the actual letters. Apply the command* Select>**Inverse** *to change the selection to the lettering. Some parts of the background will be included but this doesn't matter. Cut and paste this into a new layer and apply a Gaussian Blur filter. Place this layer below the layer that you copied so that the sharp version sits over the blurred layer.*

5 *Adjust the position of the lettering. In a separate document write a large, elegant letter. Make any corrections to the design. Copy and paste it into the original document. Adjust the size to contrast with the pattern of lettering that you first created (see pages 58–59).*

6 *Apply a Drop Shadow (or other Style that you think fits) to the large letter. Readjust the juxtaposition of each of the calligraphic elements, if necessary.*

7 *Save the design in a format that can be read as a desktop. Using JPEG will retain the full colour spectrum. In the control panel choose your design as the desktop and adjust the position of your program and other icons.*

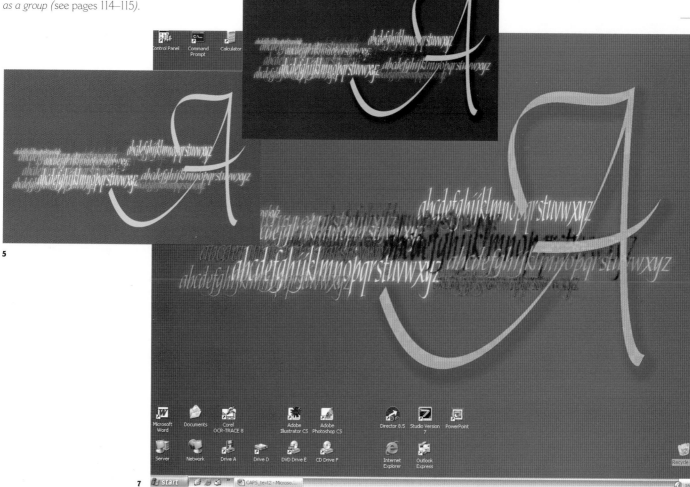

Writing calligraphy with a traditional pen and ink on paper, scanning it, then importing it into Photoshop overcomes the problem of creating text of more than a few words. Your calligraphy doesn't have to be highly skilled to be effective once modifications have been made to it through vector adjustments, filters, and other effects. Obviously, the more accomplished your calligraphy, the greater the scope for working with it. All of the elements in this example are imported from work on paper.

An Autumn eve
See the valley mists arise
Among the fir leaves
That still hold the dripping wet
Of the chill day's sudden shower

1

SOME WORKED EXAMPLES

Using scanned calligraphy

150

An Autumn eve
See the valley mists arise
Among the fir leaves
That still hold the dripping wet
Of the chill da

2

An Autumn eve
An Autumn eve
See the valley mists arise
See the valley mists arise
Among the fir leaves
Among the fir leaves
That still hold the dripping wet
That still hold the dripping wet
Of the chill day's sudden shower
Of the chill day's sudden shower

3

1 *Write the text that you want to use on paper in black ink. You can use very formal calligraphy or something more akin to free handwriting. Scan it at high resolution and save the file. Write the text again in a different calligraphic style, ideally using a different pen size to create lettering of a very different weight. Scan it and save it to file. Start a new Photoshop document and import the first file into a new active layer.*

2 *Make the background black. Colour the lettering with the* Paint Bucket *tool or by using a* Color Overlay *(Layers palette). Make the weight of the lettering heavier (bolder) by applying a soft-edged* Stroke *to the outside.*

3 *Duplicate the layer with the lettering and drag it to a position between the lines of the original lettered layer. Don't worry if the letters overlap. Merge the two layers.*

4

One of the easiest ways of creating an effective piece of calligraphy work in Photoshop is to use some lettering as a pale or obscure background with another piece of crisp, clear lettering overlaid on it. Copying and pasting text repeatedly can build up an interesting textured background very quickly. Be careful that any background lettering doesn't affect the legibility of any text you want to be read easily. This can be controlled through adjustments to opacity. In this example the textural background is on black. Bright colours on black can be striking. Medieval stained glass is a good illustration of this. However, do try using more subdued colours when the subject demands it. Here the colours are not the obvious browns and yellows of fall but are intended to reflect the feeling of chill mentioned in the poem.

4 *Apply a drop shadow the same colour as the lettering but with 0 pixels distance so that the effect is to soften the edges of the calligraphy further. Adjust the opacity of the layer so that it merges somewhat into the background (see pages 90–91).*

5 *Import the lettering in the different style from the second file that you saved. Make the colour white (or another very light colour depending on your design) and, using a transformation, scale it to sit over the background lettering.*

6 *As the text is a translation from a piece of Japanese verse, we will incorporate a Japanese character into the design. Draw or trace a suitable character (or any other appropriate illustration), then scan, and import it into your document. Adjust the colour, scale, and opacity to work with your design. Make sure that you position the layer so that it doesn't obscure any of the main calligraphic text. You can apply a filter or style, but it has been left very simple in this illustration.*

5

6

Poetry is a very popular subject for calligraphy but it is often one of the most difficult to plan and design because it has a predefined structure. When the verses are simple and of equal length the problem is not so great. Our example is an Elizabethan poem with five verses, each with eight lines. It has quaint spelling and unfamiliar words, which are typical of the period. The verses of the poetry will be typographic since it would be impractical to create this amount of text calligraphically in Photoshop. The calligraphy will be restricted to the initial letters. A coloured background will have some abstract shapes added to create interest. The colours themselves will be very subtle to help retain a unity throughout the design.

Elizabethan verse

1 *Start a new document, landscape format, and colour the background in a midtone neutral colour. On a separate layer paint a rectangular shape in a colour and tone similar but slightly different from the background. Use a brush that gives an irregular edge, like torn paper. Don't try to be too precise, and leave more space at the top than at the bottom (see pages 20–21).*

2 *Divide the page into a number of columns equal to the number of verses in the poem you have chosen. Leave small channels between the columns. Draw guides from the rulers. Add a horizontal guide for the top line of the text that you will key in.*

3 *Type the text of each verse in any colour and fit them within the columns. Make sure that you have the paragraph setting at* Left Align Text *and not* Justified. *If the column width is not enough to accommodate your line length, reduce the point size.*

1

2

3a

Hey! now the day dawis;
The jolly cock crawis;
Now shroudis the shawis
Thro' Nature anon,
The thissel-cock cryis
On lovers wha lyis;
Now skaillis the skyis;
The nicht is neir gone.

The fieldis ouerflowis
With gowans that growis,
Quhair lilies like low is
As red as the rone,
The turtle that true is'
With notes that renewis,
Hir pairty pursuus;
The nicht is neir gone.

Now hairtis with hindis
Conform to their kindis,
Hie turnis their tyndis
On ground quhair they grane.
Now hurchonis, with hairis,
Ayr passis in pairis;
Quhilk duly declaris
The nicht is neir gone.

The frekis on feildis
That wight wapins weildis
With shyning bright shieldis
At Titan in trone.
Still speiris in reistis
Ouer corseris crestis
Are broke on their breistis;
The nicht is neir gone.

3b

Hey! now the day dawis;
The jolly cock crawis;
Now shroudis the shawis
Thro' Nature anon,
The thissel-cock cryis
On lovers wha lyis;
Now skaillis the skyis;
The nicht is neir gone.

The fieldis ouerflowis
With gowans that growis,
Quhair lilies like low is
As red as the rone,
The turtle that true is'
With notes that renewis,
Hir pairty pursuus;
The nicht is neir gone.

Now hairtis with hindis
Conform to their kindis,
Hie turnis their tyndis
On ground quhair they grane.
Now hurchonis, with hairis,
Ayr passis in pairis;
Quhilk duly declaris
The nicht is neir gone.

The frekis on feildis
That wight wapins weildis
With shyning bright shieldis
At Titan in trone.
Still speiris in reistis
Ouer corseris crestis
Are broke on their breistis;
The nicht is neir gone.

So hard are their hertis;
Some sweyis, some sittis,
And some perforce flittis
On ground quite they grane.
Syne groomis that gay is
On blankis that brayis
With swordis assayis—
The nicht is neir gone.

4

4 With the same or a similar brush to that with which you painted the large rectangle, and in a slightly different colour from the background, paint a number of rough rectangles in the spaces above each verse of the poem. It is probably best to remove the guides at this point.

5 Using a calligraphic brush tool write the initial letter of each verse. Scale and position each within the rectangle of the second group that you painted. Merge the layers with the initial letters so that any changes made will affect all of them.

6 Try changing the colour of the initial letters and the rough rectangular background. You may get a satisfactory result but the illustrated example is rather light in visual weight and something has to be added to the letters to make them more interesting.

7 The letters can be enhanced in several ways. The style filters Outer Glow, Color Overlay, and Inner Shadow have been applied in the example.

8 The black text can now be changed to blend in better with the background. Create a suitable gradient layer style and copy it to each of the text layers. All that remains to be done now is to reposition the text and rectangular backgrounds. Merge all layers except the plain background and drag the calligraphy, text, and rectangles to their final position.

5

6

7

8

The aim of this exercise is to apply similar techniques and processes in a document comprising several pages, using very different effects on the lettering but trying to retain some sort of coordination throughout. It will familiarize you with some of the basic filter, transformation, and overlay procedures. The finished product could be a child's book but, with the right approach, the same principles could be applied to a more formal application such as chapter openings in a company report. Multiple style filters are used together and the effect of each controlled by adjustments to opacity.

A multipage document

1 *Open a new document letter size (11 inches by 8½ inches) and portrait orientation. Name it 'Number 1'. A typeface will be used for the numeral. Use guides to keep the numerals and the numbers spelt out in words that will be used in the design to the same size. Our example has guides at one, eight, eight and a half, and ten inches from the top and a centered guide at four and a half inches from the left.*

2 *Type the first numeral. Using the Edit> Transform command, enlarge the number until it fits between the top two guidelines and centre it. Keep the same aspect ratio by holding down the Shift key while you scale the selection (see pages 58–59). Using a calligraphic brush, write the name of the number (zero for '0' in the example) between the lower two guides. As usual, a new type layer will automatically be created. Scale this lettering to fit between the lines, constraining the proportions in the same way as with the large numeral by holding down the Shift key.*

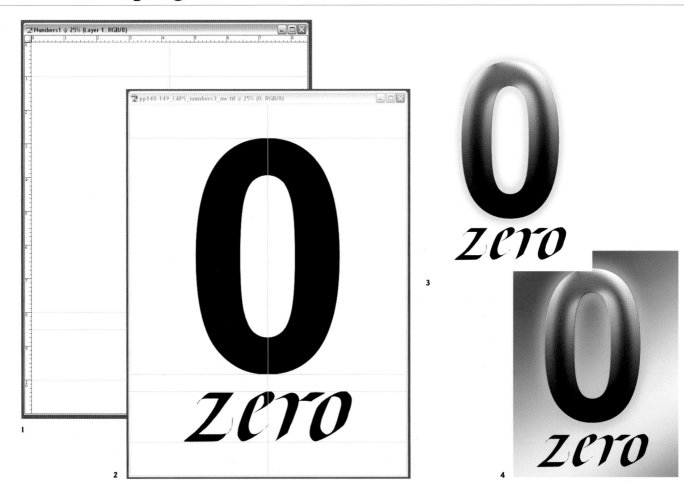

3 *Devise and apply a style filter to the large numeral. There will be an element of trial and error in this, as you won't see the final effect until later in the project. If you are unhappy with the outcome when the other layers are applied, step backward to this point and try a different filter.*

4 *In the background layer, fill the background using a simple, gradient, or style fill.*

5 *With the word layer (zero) active, select it with the Magic Wand tool, copy and paste it into a new layer. Scale the word until it is a little smaller than the page size. At this point the result is an extremely confused image.*

6 *Locate this new word layer behind the layer with the large numeral and apply a style filter to it. In the* Layers *palette, reduce the opacity of the word to 30% or less.*

7 *Make adjustments to the colour, style, and position of the first number word that you wrote so that it stands out clearly from the rest of the design. Repeat the process for the other nine numerals, creating new documents named Numbers 2 to 10, keeping the calligraphic style the same as far as possible, but using different colours and layer styles.*

8 *Create a new document large enough to take your designs one to nine. Zero can be omitted to keep the shape regular. Paste the pages into this document to see how well your choice of colours and filters are coordinated.*

5

6

7

8

There is a wealth of books on traditional calligraphy but very few on the use of graphics software for lettering. Some of the publications listed are no longer in print but worth seeking out in a library or from www.abebooks.com. Computer software manuals tend to give the impression that they are written by computer experts for computer experts. There are several good guides to the use of Photoshop that are easier to follow than the Adobe manual, some of which are listed here.

Bibliography & website addresses

BOOKS ON CALLIGRAPHY

Anderson, Donald M., **The Art of Written Forms: The Theory and Practice of Calligraphy** (Holt, Rinehart and Winston, New York, 1989). *A classic work that deals with historical and contemporary calligraphy and lettering.*

Child, Heather, **Calligraphy Today. Twentieth-Century Tradition and Practice** (Taplinger, New York, 1988). *Although this book is rather dated, it still includes many good illustrations of calligraphy in practice.*

Daubney, Margaret, **Calligraphy** (Crowood, Marlborough, 2000). *This is a good practical guide.*

De Hamel, Christopher, **A History of the Illuminated Manuscript** (Phaidon, Oxford, 1994). *A major work with a large number of superb illustrations of medieval manuscripts as well as an authoritative text.*

Diringer, David, **The Alphabet** (Hutchinson, London, 1968). *The classic work on the history of writing. It deals with both Western and Eastern scripts.*

Drogan, Marc, **Medieval Calligraphy. Its History and Technique** (Dover, New York, 1989). *A good practical guide for those who want to base their calligraphy firmly on historical styles.*

Gray, Nicolete, **A History of Lettering** (Phaidon, London, 1986). *Gray is one of the most readable authors on the subject of lettering. This is a good detailed history.*

Halliday, Peter (ed.), **Calligraphy Masterclass** (Bloomsbury, London, 1995). *This volume is full of inspirational ideas for calligraphy.*

Halliday, Peter, **Calligraphy. Art and Colour** (Batsford, London, 1994). *A practical guide to the use of colour in calligraphy.*

Harvey, Michael, **Creative Lettering Today** (A. & C. Black, London, 1996). *This book includes a section on computer type design.*

Jackson, Donald, **The Story of Writing** (The Calligraphy Centre, Monmouth, UK, 1994). *Another classic work on the history of calligraphic lettering.*

Thomson, George, **Digital Calligraphy. How to Create Perfect Lettering from Your Desktop** (Watson-Guptill, New York, 2003). *The only book on digital calligraphy.*

Thomson, George, **The Calligraphy Kit** (Chronicle, San Francisco, 2003). *A short, clear guide to calligraphic technique, together with the basic materials to get started.*

BOOKS ON PHOTOSHOP

Adobe, **Adobe Photoshop CS. Classroom in a Book. The Official Training Workbook from Adobe Systems** (Adobe/Peachpit, Berkeley, 2004). *An up-to-date official guide to Photoshop CS.*

McClelland, Deke, **Photoshop CS Bible** (Wiley, New York, 2004). *This is an easy-to-understand guide to Photoshop.*

WEBSITES

Societies and other organizations

Association for the Calligraphic Arts (US)
www.calligraphicarts.org

Atlanta Friends of the Alphabet (US)
www.friendsofthealphabet.org

Calligraphy and Lettering Arts Society (UK)
www.clas.co.uk

Calligraphy Societies of Florida (US)
www.calligraphers.com/florida

Carolina Lettering Arts Society (US)
www.carolinaletteringarts.com

New York Society of Scribes (US)
www.societyofscribes.org

Society of Scribes and Illuminators (UK)
www.calligraphyonline.org

Washington Calligraphers' Guild
www.calligraphersguild.org

Homepages of calligraphers

Denis Brown
www.geocities.com/denisbrown72

Michael Clark
www.ideabook.com/michaelclark

Timothy Donaldson
www.timothydonaldson.com

Gerald Fleuss, Patricia Gidney, and Susan Hufton
www.calligraphyanddesign.com

Ray Ritchie
www.rritchie.com

George Thomson
http://dspace.dial.pipex.com/georgethomson

Dave Wood
www.davewood.com.au

Other websites

Cyberscribes bulletin board
www.calligraph.com/callig

Cynscribe
www.cynscribe.com

The Edward Johnston Foundation (UK)
www.letteringtoday.co.uk/ejfhome.html

We learn to read, in various languages, in various sciences; we learn the alphabet and letters of all manner of Books. But the place where we are to get knowledge, even theoretic knowledge, is the Books themselves!

Thomas Carlyle 1840